PIPER TUNING MANUAL

Bob Gayler

CAUTION!

When the power output of any engine is increased, the owner should ensure that the braking and suspension capabilities of the vehicle are uprated to accomodate its increased performance.

It will also be necessary to notify the vehicle's insurers of any modifications which change its performance capabilities from that of the standard model.

Whilst every effort has been made to ensure the accuracy of the information given in this manual no liability can be accepted by the author or publisher for loss, damage or injury caused by errors in, or omissions from, the information given.

ISBN 0 85429 292 6

© R.J.(Bob) Gayler/Piper FM Ltd 1981

First published 1981

All rights reserved. No part of this book may be reproduced or transmitted in any form or by any means electronic or mechanical, including photocopying, recording or by any information storage or retrieval system, without permission of the publisher.

A FOULIS Book

Published by
Haynes Publishing Group
Sparkford, Yeovil, Somerset BA22 7JJ, England

Distributed in North America by
Haynes Publications Inc
861 Lawrence Drive, Newbury Park,
California 91320 USA

Editor Rod Grainger
Dust jacket design Phil Jennings
Printed and bound in England by Haynes Publishing Group
This title produced in association with Piper FM Ltd,
Bromley Green Road, Ashford, Kent TN26 2EF.

Contents

Chapter 1: Power! 5
Horsepower... what is it? 5
Measuring horsepower 6
The dynamometer 7
What controls power? How can it be improved? 8
The four-stroke chain of power 10
The two-stroke chain of power 10

Chapter 2: Breathing 11
Air boxes and cleaners 11
Carburettors 12
Carburettor selection 13
Fuel-injection, the alternative 14
Inlet ports and valves 16
Inlet valve timing (four-stroke) 17
Two-stroke port timing 17
Camshaft choice 18
Camshaft regrinding – does it work? 19
Camshaft position and drive 20
Camshaft installation 21
Camshaft – checking and setting timing 22
Two-stroke port timing – checking and modification 25
Combustion – the power stroke 26
The exhaust system – Four-stroke 27
The exhaust system – Two-stroke 29

Chapter 3: Ignition 31
Is ignition advance necessary? 31
Selecting a suitable advance curve 32
Electronic ignition 33
Spark plugs – selection and mixture checking 33

Chapter 4: Turbocharger or Supercharger? 35
Fitting a Turbocharger/Supercharger 36
Engine modifications for Turbocharging/Supercharging 36
Camshafts for Turbocharged/Supercharged engines 37

Chapter 5: Engine Survival 39
Valves – quality check 39
O.H.V. engines 39
O.H.C. engines 39
Valve to valve and valve to piston clearance, hemispherical combustion chambers 40
Combustion chamber 40
Detonation 40
Deck height 40
Pistons and rings 40
Connecting rods 41
Crankshafts 42
Flywheel lightening 43
Balancing 43
Assembly hints 43

Introduction

The New Piper Tuning Manual is a concise collection of vital facts and figures, intended as a working basis for anyone intent on serious engine tuning or modification. The information is based on the cumulative results of ten years of intensive engine reworking and testing in the Piper workshops, and covers a range of engines from small two-strokes through to V12 four-strokes.

Information is presented in a manner as 'painless' as possible, and where it is necessary to present a formula to enable calculation of an individual function it is reduced to the minimum number of variables which are, themselves, carefully explained.

Do not be misled by the manual's small size. Explanations of the phenomena that occur in the internal combustion engine have purposely been reduced to an absolute minimum, in order to concentrate on the 'nuts and bolts' of efficient tuning. Similarly, it has been assumed that the reader has a basic working knowledge of engine parts and processes and therefore space has not been wasted on the ordinary tuning processes of standard or mildly modified engines. These are adequately covered in many other publications.

The author, Bob Gayler, is the Technical Director of Piper Cams, and has been concerned with the theoretical and practical aspects of engine development for over twenty years. He is a trained engineer with 'bitter experience' knowledge of the daily problems that beset the practical tuner. He understands that scientific explanations of the various engine processes are important, and enjoyed by the student, but that they can tend to cloud the 'grass-roots' information that gets the engine screwed together fast and reliably. On the other hand, to achieve this result with confidence, it is necessary to understand some of the functions more deeply than others and, with this thought in mind, the content of the manual has been very carefully compiled to achieve a balance.

Chapter 1
Power!

Horsepower ... What is it?

Wherever people gather to talk motoring, motorcycling or motorsport of any kind it is only a matter of time before the word 'power' comes into the conversation. But very few people really understand what horsepower is.

The dictionary definition is 'a unit to measure the rate of doing work' — not a lot of help to someone trying to make the decision on how to tune an engine!

But every rider and driver knows the feel of power, as the throttle is opened and the clutch dropped and suddenly the wheels are spinning — that's big power.

Or when the lights turn green and you wind the twist grip of your 50cc moped, it's power that gets you moving, even though it's not quite so big.

In fact, nothing moves without power — clockwork toys, elastic bands, human beings on bicycles, all need power, large or small, to move at all. A falling stone gets its motive power from the kinetic energy imparted when someone or something lifted it against the pull of gravity. So power can also be defined as the result of converting work into movement.

The internal combustion engine is one of the most convenient ways of producing movement. All you need to do is pour in fuel at one end, pull the right knobs and levers and instant power comes out of the other end. The engine thus converts fuel into movement.

But what, *exactly*, is fuel? Fuel is neatly packaged heat — anything that burns when a match is applied is potentially capable of producing power. In this case, gasoline or methanol.

So the engine is a heat converter and, of course, this is why, when this subject is studied in college, it is entitled 'Heat Engines'. Two-stroke or four-stroke, one cylinder or sixteen, the conversion process is always carried out in the same way — by drawing in a mixture of fuel and air, compressing it, igniting it and using the resultant combustion to drive a piston down and rotate a crank.

When the engine converts fuel into power, the process is rather inefficient and only about a quarter of the potential energy in the fuel is realised as power at the flywheel. The rest is wasted as heat going down the exhaust and into the air or water. The ratio of actual to potential power is called the *thermal efficiency* of the engine.

The machine we use to measure engine performance is a *dynamometer* (see P5) and the way that it works is closely tied to the explanation of power.

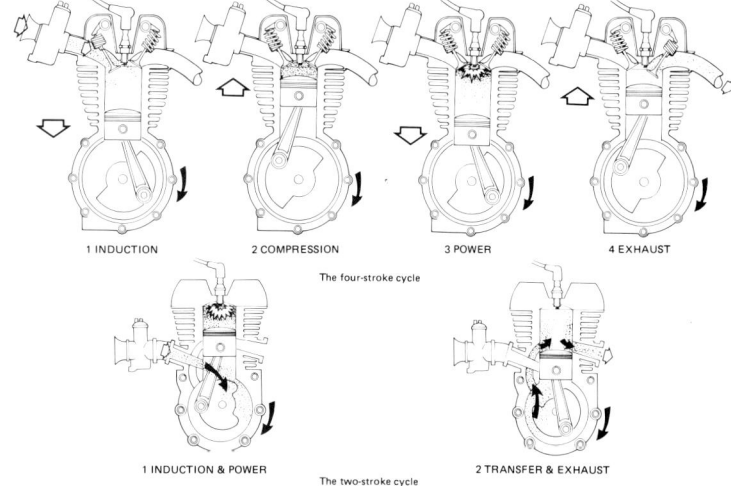

D1. 4-stroke and 2-stroke cycles.

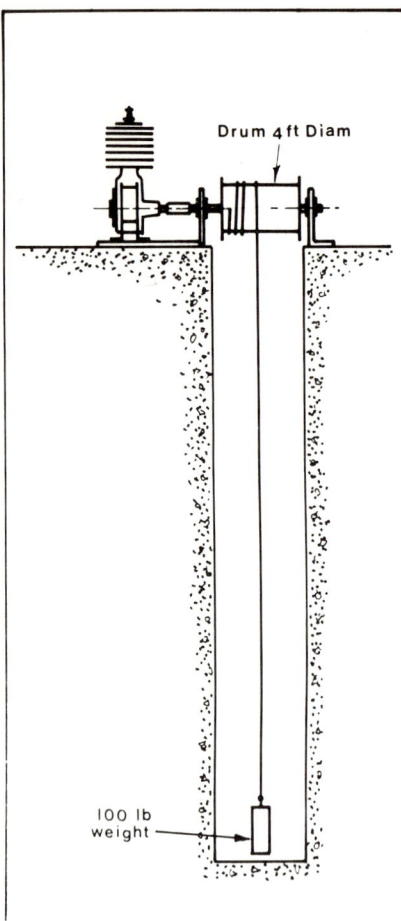

D2. Dynamometer operating principle.

5. Formula Ford engine on 'Go-Power' dyno.

Measuring horsepower

Engine power is usually described as *B.H.P* which is the abbreviation of *Brake Horse Power* and describes the power that is actually measured at the flywheel. A dynamometer does not show *B.H.P* as a direct reading, but measures *Torque* and *R.P.M* and power is calculated from these.

Torque is the amount of work that an engine is actually doing (the turning force being exerted) and is measured in *Foot-Pounds* or *Metre-Kilograms* or *Newtons* depending on whether you are using Imperial British measurement or the recently introduced International Metric System. As results obtained in the Piper workshops use the British system, we'll explain it in *Ft.lbs*.

Imagine an engine sited at the top of a deep well turning a drum which is 4 ft in diameter. A rope attached to the drum is hanging down the well with a weight of 100lbs on the end. (See diagram). As the engine turns the drum it will lift the weight. The drum is 4ft in diameter and the rope is being pulled in at 2ft from the centre of rotation; therefore, the work being done or *torque* is measured as 2ft x 100lbs, that is 200ft.lbs.

The speed at which the drum is rotating is measured as Revolutions Per Minute (R.P.M).
B.H.P. is calculated as follows:

$$\text{B.H.P.} = \frac{\text{Torque} \times \text{R.P.M.}}{\text{Constant}}$$

The constant depends on the units of torque which are being measured. As we are using ft.lbs, it will be 5250, so if we say that the engine is turning at 1000 R.P.M. then:

$$\text{B.H.P.} = \frac{200 \times 1000}{5250} = 38$$

Because we cannot calculate B.H.P. without knowing the R.P.M., it means that B.H.P. is a measure of the speed at which work is done as previously mentioned, 'a unit to measure the rate of doing work'.

To understand the way in which the dynamometer works, imagine anchoring a spring balance to the ground, with a rope attached to the top eye and wrapped around a drum with a slip knot. If the slip knot is tightened as the drum is rotating, the rope will be tensioned and the balance will extend to indicate this tension as 'weight'. As the knot is further tightened, friction between rope and drum will slow the drum and its driving engine until, at 1000 R.P.M., the spring balance reads 100 lbs.

The weight being lifted is 100lbs; the speed of the drum or engine will then be used in the formula to calculate the horsepower.

If the speed of the engine/drum were 1000 R.P.M. the B.H.P. being exerted would be 38. If the speed were 1500 R.P.M. this would mean the engine was lifting the weight faster and exerting more power to do it. The calculation would then be:

$$\frac{200 \times 1500}{5250} = 57 \text{ B.H.P.}$$

6. Racing Imp: small and light but highly competitive against bigger engined cars.

7. Full race Escort. No quicker than Imp on twisty circuits.

8. 250cc racing Yamaha in action.

9. 1000cc Honda in racing trim.

The dynamometer

So a piece of rope, a spring balance, a rev counter and the engine fitted with a flywheel or drum to take the rope is all you need to make a dynamometer. Yes — but! If the throttle is wide open and nothing's moving, where is all the power going? The answer is, that it's turning back into heat again. Where? You've guessed it! Between the drum and the rope — as friction. So, although the idea of the cheap dyno sounds good, in fact, the power being used, turning into friction heat, would set fire to the whole lot. Unless, of course, we cool it by pouring water over it, and that's just what the modern dynamometer does. It uses a device like the torque-converter of an automatic transmission to do the job of the rope and drum and is running in a continuous flow of cooled water to absorb the heat. The engine turns the inner part of the torque-converter and the water drag thus created tries to turn the outer casing, which is coupled to a big accurate weighing machine reading torque. (See diagram).

Now that we understand the meaning of power and how to measure it, just how important is it? Does an increase in power automatically mean higher speeds? Not necessarily, as the pictures give evidence. The Imp in P.6, and the Yamaha in P.8, consistently lapped faster than their bigger powered brothers in P.7 and P.9, indicating that power is only of value when applied with suitable engineering skill. Smooth, controllable power will often return better results than ultimate B.H.P. peaking over a narrow rev band.

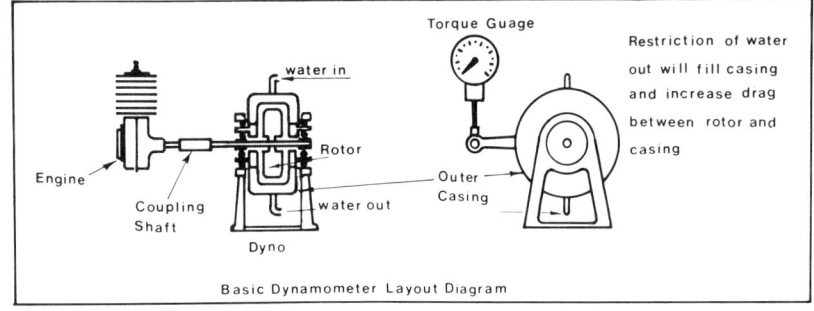

D3. Dynamometer cutaway showing function.

Piper Tuning Manual

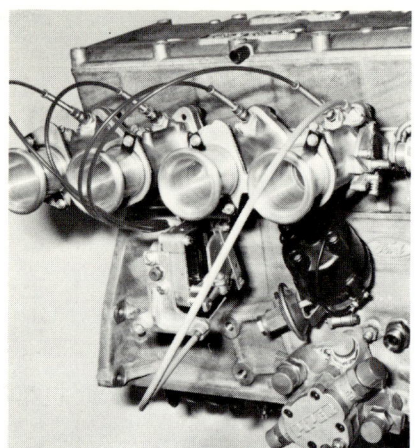

10. Production engine modified for racing.

11. Standard road Honda 750.

12. Race prepared Honda 750.

What controls the power? How can it be improved?

An engine works very much like a human being. It takes in air and fuel (food). It burns the fuel (digestion). It converts the energy released into power (muscles). Discharge of exhaust (bowels). Oil pump and circulation (heart). Cooling system (pores). Pistons and cylinders (lungs). The camshaft (brain) co-ordinates the whole sequence of operation in the same way as the brain. The efficiency of these individual functions affects engine performance in the same way that they would affect a human. Poor or contaminated fuel will have a low energy content. Bad ignition or combustion chamber shapes will reduce the ability to digest the fuel fully, resulting in an unpleasant and dirty exhaust. Clogged or inadequate oil filters or a worn oil pump will result in component failure. A dirty cooling system with clogged radiator pores will result in overheating. A poorly designed camshaft will result in erratic breathing. They all work together to produce the final flywheel muscle power, however good or bad.

To understand the process we'll start with the breathing cycle. If we think of the engine as an air pump then theoretically it should draw in and exhaust its own volume of air each time it cycles — that is, once every revolution if it's a two-stroke and once every two revolutions if it's a four-stroke. In fact, ordinary production engines don't achieve this and only manage to shift about 80% of their volume.

This ratio of possible air pumped to actual air pumped is called *Volumetric Efficiency* and this is what we have to improve to get more power. The difference in appearance between two engines of similar type, one of which is in standard road trim and one in full race trim can be seen on the left. P.11 is a standard street Honda 750 Four and P.12 is a full race version of the same model. The noticeable external differences in the engine preparation are to increase the volumetric efficiency.

Volumetric efficiency = breathing ability = power! The breathing cycle is controlled by a chain of parts, each one of which depends on the others to work at its best.

The process starts at the air cleaner which varies from being a large box containing a large paper filtration and silencing element, necessary for silent operation and engine protection under a variety of dusty and sandy conditions, through to the light and minimal filters of rally cars and speedway bikes, to the completely open bellmouths of full circuit racing machines.

The next link in the chain is carburation. The process of mixing the fuel and air and feeding them to the engine in balanced doses, that is, about fifteen times as much air as fuel. Fifteen to one — air/fuel ratio — another important controller in final power output!

Although we call it 'carburation', here it can also include fuel-injection, just another method of delivering fuel to the engine.

So, via inlet manifolds or stubs we move to the next link and here is where the *Two-Stroke* and *Four-Stroke* engines divide.

Piper Tuning Manual

13. Honda moped 4-stroke engine.

14. Piper P.80 2-stroke engine on dyno.

15. Ford-Cosworth DFV F2 engine showing exhaust and intake system.

16. Close-up of Suzuki's GT750 2-stroke engine.

```
          FOUR-STROKE                TWO-STROKE
                └───────────┬───────────┘
                            │
                   AIR BOX OR CLEANER
                            │
                        RAM-PIPE
                            │
                      CARBURETTOR
                            │
                    FUEL-INJECTION
                            │
                     INLET MANIFOLD
                            │
                ┌───────────┴───────────┐
         CYLINDER-HEAD              CRANK-CASE
                │                       │
             PORTING                PISTON VALVE
                │                       │
          INLET VALVE           PISTON SUPERCHARGER
                │                       │
           CAMSHAFT              TRANSFER TIMING
                └───────────┬───────────┘
```

COMBUSTION !

```
                ┌───────────┴───────────┐
        EXHAUST VALVE            EXHAUST PORT TIMING
                │                       │
         SIMPLE PARALLEL          COMPLEX MULTI-
      PIPE EXHAUST SYSTEM.       TAPER SYSTEM, ONLY
       COUPLED WITH MULTI-        COUPLED WITH 3
        CYLINDER ENGINES             CYLINDERS
                │                       │
         POSSIBLY A SIMPLE       EXPANSION CHAMBER,
            MEGAPHONE             REVERSE CONE,
                                RESTRICTIVE TAIL-PIPE

         150+ BHP/LITRE            200+ BHP/LITRE
```

D4. 4-stroke/2-stroke operation comparison.

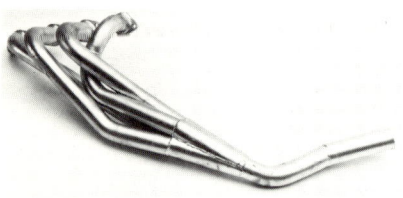

17. Camshafts for 4-cylinder production engines.

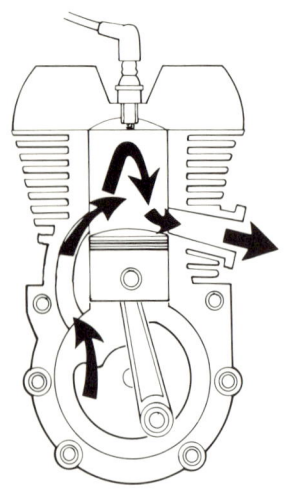

18. 4-stroke 4-into-1 tuned exhaust manifold.

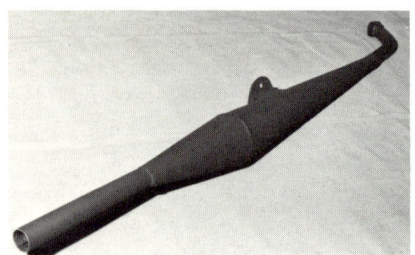

D5. 2-stroke transfer port operation.

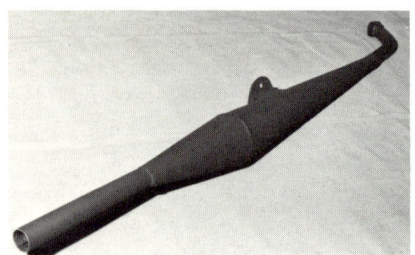

19. 2-stroke tuned exhaust.

The four-stroke chain of power

The mixture enters the cylinder head and is induced through the inlet valve into the combustion chamber. The way in which it enters the chamber is controlled by the port shape and finish and the inlet valve timing, which in turn is controlled by the camshaft.

The camshaft is probably the most important single component in the four-stroke engine, as far as power production is concerned, and it is certainly the most complicated piece to design and produce (P 17).

Compression takes place followed by ignition and combustion — the point at which four- and two-stroke re-unite in a common process.

Exhaust is again controlled by the camshaft operating the exhaust valve, in a four-stroke engine, and then by the design of the port and the exhaust system which, in turn, has a considerable effect on exhaust efficiency (P.18).

The two-stroke chain of power

There are several ways in which the two-stroke engine will work but we will consider only the modern loop-scavenge design which is the most commonly used production version.

As the piston rises, a depression is created in the crankcase and the mixture is drawn in at the point where the piston skirt starts to uncover the inlet port. As the piston comes down, the inlet port is closed and the charge is compressed and driven up the transfer port into the combustion chamber (D.5). Because the mixture is being forced into the chamber under pressure, this is really a form of supercharging and is one of the reasons that this type of engine can produce so much power relative to its size.

As the piston rises again, compression takes place, followed by ignition and combustion, driving the piston down which opens the exhaust port and drives a new charge into the combustion chamber at the same time. Because these two happen together, the design of the transfer port and exhaust system must be just right in order to clear the foul gas and ensure a full charge of new mixture without wasting any down the exhaust port (P.19).

Although the two designs appear to be very different, the overall function of both is the same — fuel into power, the level of which is governed by volumetric efficiency.

The significant part of the chart on page 9 is the point where the two engines coincide at *combustion*. The key to high power output is fast, controlled, near total burning of the compressed mixture. This key is common to all types of internal combustion engine and is dependent on all the parts around it.

Now we'll start looking at those parts in detail.

Chapter 2
Breathing

20. *Standard production air cleaner with remote air entry point.*

21. *Air entry scoop on dragster car.*

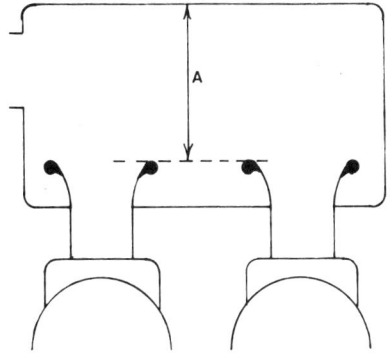

D6. *Ram-pipe ends in airbox.*

22. *Standard air cleaners and air feed to carbs, Yamaha 250.*

Air boxes and cleaners

The need to use an air box at all must be judged by the environment surrounding the engine and in which the vehicle is going to be used.

For example, while it is unlikely that a motor cycle will need any additional cold air fed into the carbs, the engine compartment of a car is often very hot and poorly ventilated, so the argument for an airbox here is to get cold air from the front of the car, under the bonnet to the carbs. (P.20 and P.21).

On the other hand, if the bike or car is going to be used in excessively dusty or sandy conditions, then an air box and filter are essential.

General rule of thumb is that vehicles used for pure circuit work or fast road work, including dragsters, in Europe, can do without any box at all except for during the occasional long hot summer when the dust level is high. This supposes that you are prepared to put up with the induction roar of unsilenced intakes. Autocross, rally, dirt and grasstrack vehicles all need boxes.

The important thing is to apply the air box in the right way. It should be the point at which the induction pulse can expand in the same way as if there were no box there at all, *ie* the bellmouths should be allowed to protrude into the box with adequate clearance, (see D.6) and 'A' should be at least as great as the carburettor bore size.

Tubular couplings as in P.22 will effectively increase the tuned ram length to an rpm level that will probably be too low.

Ram length is the tuned length from the inlet valve head or piston port face to the end of the intake trumpet. When the valve or port first cracks open a pressure wave travels up and down the inlet tract changing from plus pressure to minus pressure, or suction. If it is caught at the right time it can be used to help ram mixture into the engine.

You can calculate approximate correct ram length using the formula below. (L = length).

For a four-stroke:

$$L \text{ in inches.} = \frac{228 \times T}{N}$$

Where T = Inlet valve timing in degrees
N = The estimated rpm at which max. power will be achieved minus five hundred.

and for a two-stroke:

$$L \text{ in inches.} = \frac{1150 \times T}{N}$$

Where T = Inlet valve timing in degrees
N = The estimated rpm at which max. power will be achieved.

This will result in a length that is too great to be practical and can be divided by 3 or 5 to fit installation requirements.

Ram pipes or trumpets should have fully rounded ends as in D.6 because, contrary to general belief, much of the air is drawn in around these ends and if there are sharp edges in this area, flow will be interrupted and turbulence will cause restriction in the bellmouth. This is also the reason why the bellmouth should be allowed to protrude into the air box rather than finish flush with the wall. The position of the air entry to the box is not critical provided it is not within two inches of any of the bellmouths.

Carburettors

The process of improving volumetric efficiency is invariably tied up with an increase in the operating rpm of the engine in order to increase power. However, if we increase rpm, then we will inevitably be increasing the air speed in the inlet tract, which includes the carburettor. The size of carburettor that is normally suitable for the standard engine, is rarely large enough for any appreciable increase in the state of tune other than Stage I. Stage I modifications vary from one engine to another but generally comprise a mild increase in cam profile on a four-stroke or lengthening of inlet and exhaust timings by about 5° on a two-stroke, raising compression by about one ratio, smoothing out porting and possibly fitting a higher performance exhaust system. Even at this level the engine can easily be strangled by its standard carbs. So any further increase means that we are inevitably faced with the need to uprate the carburation. To evaluate the European options available, we will first divide them into types depending on their principle of operation:

1. Fixed choke, butterfly air control.
   Weber and Dellorto
   Other fixed choke carburettors are available but are impractical due to lack of ability to be variably adjusted.

2. Variable choke, butterfly air control, constant depression (C.D.).
   S.U., Stromberg C.D., Mikuni, not generally used for two-stroke application.

3. Variable choke, manual slide control of air and fuel.
   Amal, Keihin, Mikuni, Lectron, Gardner, Dellorto.

23. Keihin carbs on a Kawasaki 1000.

24. Amal carbs fitted to a Honda 250.

Suitability and convenience of application:

1. *Weber* – D.C.O.E. series sidedraught (P.25).
   – I.D.A. and D.C.N. series downdraught.
   Size range from 38mm to 48mm.
   Without doubt the best high performance carburettor available in the world for application in cars. Wide range of chokes and jets readily available for applying to any engine. Usable for motorcycles but rather big and bulky for average application, also needs special fuel delivery requirements, *ie* pump delivery or modified needle valves.

2. *Dellorto* – D.H.L.A. series sidedraught.
   – F.Z.D. series sidedraught.
   Size range from 20mm to 48mm.
   D.H.L.A. series similar to Weber D.C.O.E. but not quite as efficient in terms of airflow. Not quite the same range of variables available. Other series are readily adaptable to motor cycle applications.

3. *S.U* – Size range from $1\frac{1}{4}$ in. to 2 in. (P.26)
   The most widely used high performance carburettor up to the 70s. Still very popular for road conversions.
   Very adaptable, wide range of needles available, tend to suffer fuel surge on high cornering G-forces.

4. *Stromberg C.D.* – Size range from $1\frac{1}{4}$ in. to $1\frac{3}{4}$ in.
   Similar in operation to S.U. Not such a wide range of needles. Application not quite so simple.

5. *Mikuni and Keihin (P.23)* – Both make C.D carburettors for use on road bikes and also make manual slide control versions for use on racing bikes. They are available as kits for some production models but generally, they are difficult to apply to other models due to lack of non-standard jets and needles. Properly set up, they make efficient and reliable racing carburation.

6. *Amal (P.24)* – Size range 25mm–42mm.
The most popular and successful motorcycle carburettor for many years. Very adaptable to almost any engine and very forgiving to slight errors in tuning.

7. *Gardner and Lectron.*
Similar operation with manually operated flat slide and unique tapered needles with machined flat surface down its length. Gardner has no float chamber and meters fuel direct from gravity head in tank. Generally used for speedway, grass track and dragster single cylinder machines. Lectron has concentric float chamber which makes it more adaptable.

All carburettors, whatever the make, suffer, to a degree, from two major faults – fuel frothing due to vibration and float chamber fuel surge due to cornering G-forces. In many cases these can be minimised by careful attention to flexible mountings, float levels, needle valves and springs where applicable.

25. Weber carbs on a race prepared Toyota.

26. SU carbs on Rover V8.

Carburettor selection

Refer to the camshaft selection table on page 23 for Stage descriptions.

Stage 1: There is no real point in modifying even slightly if the standard engine is not of the GT type, which is really the manufacturer's first mild production tuning step from his basic engine. Carburation at this stage will generally be two small C.D.s or a single progressive twin-choke which will only need needle or jet changes for Stage 1.

Stage 2: Increase in volumetric efficiency at this point will call for an increase in size of C.D. carbs. (*eg* 1300cc engine running on 2 x 1¼ inch S.U.s will need to move up to 1½ inch units. Or will need a large choke version of twin-choke DD carb.). Also will need a change of air cleaners to freeflow type. At this stage single choke injection systems can be considered as a possible alternative.

Stage 3: Further volumetric efficiency improvements now create a 'grey area' in which well-engineered twin carbs, or single choke injection, will still do the required job, but the move toward one choke per cylinder must be seriously considered. Cylinder sizes up to 400cc will require a 40mm carburettor with 30 to 34mm chokes fitted (*eg* Ford 1300cc four cylinder will need 2 X 40DCOE Weber or DHLA Dellorto).

Stage 4: One choke per cylinder is now essential to fully justify other engine modifications. Available choices are Weber DCOE, Dellorto DHLA, Amal, Keihin or Mikuni smooth bores.

27. Injection system fitted to Jaguar V12.

28. Piper injection on Kawasaki 1000, showing part of fuel control system.

29. Airflow sensing device on Bosch 'K' injection.

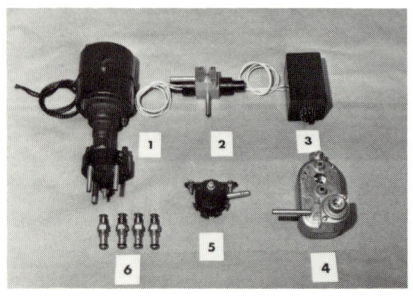

30. Piper-RDA injection system components.

Carburettor sizes will need to be as follows for various cylinder sizes:
250cc. 40mm with 32-34mm choke or injection bore.
400cc. 45mm with 36-40mm choke or injection bore.
500cc. 48-52mm with 40-46mm choke or injection bore.

Stage 5/ Stage 6: As above except that we now move into the area where individual engine build specifications will dictate precise intake breathing requirements, and it is no longer possible to predict general sizes. Only dynamometer testing of the engine build combinations will produce the most effective results from carburation or injection variants.

At best, initial carburation choice can only be a compromise generally suited to the user's overall requirements and will eventually have to be adjusted accordingly. Genuine designers and suppliers of good high performance equipment will be able to advise you on jet settings for your individual needs. Beware of buying cheap unrelated tuning parts; nobody will be prepared to advise you on the finer tuning details needed to complete a satisfactory job.

Fuel-injection, the alternative

'Fuel-injection' should describe the process of injection directly into the combustion chamber in the same way that a diesel engine functions. The last engine of any note to do this was the Mercedes 300SL and the practice has now been discarded due to impracticality and high cost. Present day injection systems squirt fuel into the inlet manifold or cylinder head close to the inlet valve. They are really a form of carburation or 'pressurised fuel metering systems.'

All injection systems work on the same basic principle. A series of signals from the engine are registered and used to produce a squirt of fuel of the correct size at the correct time. The important signals that need to be measured are:

1. *Engine speed* — measured either by a mechanical pump driven directly from the crankshaft and increasing its fuel delivery as the speed rises, or sensed electronically and fed into a circuit board to control an electro/mechanical fuel metering device.

2. *Throttle opening* — measured either mechanically or electrically and indicating the driver's power call-off from the engine at any time, *eg* the sudden change from one eighth open to full open indicates driver requirement for sudden acceleration and therefore mixture richness is fed in accordingly.

3. *Engine air consumption or volumetric efficiency.* A big thorn in the side of injection equipment designers. Eventually it will be measured electronically as the state of the art develops, but in the infant years of fuel-injection it is measured mechanically by use of manifold pressure sensing devices or by a 'floating' air bell (P.29) in the induction tract. This is very sensitive but can be subject to problems of dirt deposits causing 'sticky' operation. It is also difficult to modify when the engine is uprated because it is critical in design and in itself offers an obstruction to clean airflow.

Various other controls are introduced depending on the sophistication of the system or the individual quirks of the designer. Such devices, as atmospheric pressure, temperature and exhaust gas analysis sensors, feed signals to a simple mini-computer which, in turn, tells the metering system to

31. Piper-RDA injection for marine Rover V8 engine.

32. Rover V8 injection kit from Piper.

33. Ford Fiesta with Piper-RDA injection.

34. Avenger engine fitted with Piper injection.

correct the fuel flow accordingly. But whether or not they use these additions, all systems have to work around the three basic control parameters listed above.

Most injection systems are purpose-designed for the vehicle to which they are fitted and are difficult to re-adapt for other engines. The Lucas system as used on Formula 1 and 2 cars is available in component form for use on any engine, but the responsibility for adapting and fitting, including determination of the control cam shape to suit fuel requirements, lies with the customer, a formidable task for anyone who does not have expensive test equipment. Piper-R.D.A. manufacture a system which is readily adaptable to both cars and motorcycles by anyone with average workshop facilities. It is an electro-mechanical system (see P.30) in which an electric pump (1) takes fuel from the tank and returns it via a pressure relief valve. This creates a primary fuel circuit at a constant controlled pressure that is not subject to surge from G-forces. In the car application this incorporates a swirl-pot to de-aerate the fuel.

On motorcycles, because of the short run to and from the tank, the swirl-pot is not required. Fuel is taken from this primary circuit and fed to a solenoid pulsing valve (2). The speed at which this valve operates is controlled by the ignition coil pulse via the electronic control module (3). From here the fuel is fed to a mechanical control valve which, in turn, is linked to the throttle valves or butterflies (4).

It is then delivered via a pressure control valve and distributor block (5) to the injection nozzles (6). The system in this simple form is suitable for racing use and for road use by experienced drivers with sensitive throttle control. But where automatic part throttle control is needed for normal use in heavy traffic, an additional control is introduced which 'recognizes' volumetric efficiency at any given time and feeds a signal back into the control module.

The beauty of the whole system is that no complex cam design, involving expensive test equipment, is necessary and the mixture strength can be adjusted by a touch of a knob on the control module. An additional adjustment will alter the 'slope' of the fuel delivery so that mixture can be adjusted at one end of the rev range without altering the other end.

The table below lists the variation of driving conditions and the resulting demands put on any fuel metering system, whether carburation or injection.

Driving Condition	Throttle position	Engine speed	Volumetric efficiency	Fuel requirement
Cold start	Closed to 1/8	Low	Poor	Rich
Hot start	Ditto	Low	Poor	Weak
Cruise at 70mph on motorway flat or slight downhill	1/8	Med./High	Poor	Weak
Flat out, flat road.	Full	High	Good	Med.
Accelerate on steep hill	$\frac{1}{2}$ to full	Low	Poor	Rich
Dragster start from lights	Full	Low	Poor	Rich
Cruise at 70mph, slight uphill	$\frac{1}{2}$	Med.	Med.	Med.
Shut throttle suddenly from 150mph	Closed	High	Poor	Near zero

35. *Race prepared Norton and Ford BDA cylinder heads, showing highly polished ports.*

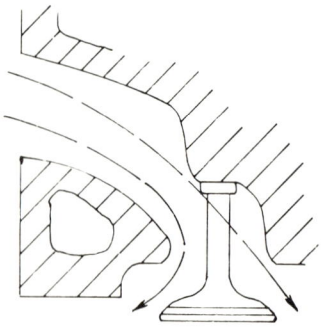

D7. *4-stroke inlet port and valve.*

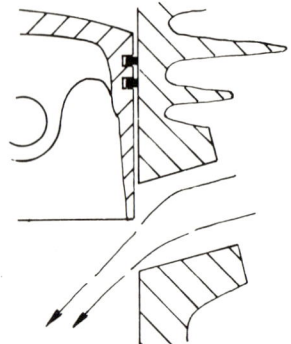

D8. *2-stroke inlet port and piston.*

The difficulty of meeting all these possible combinations makes the carburettor look good value for money and it is. However the requirements of greater economy, together with reduced exhaust emission levels, are necessitating the change to much greater sophistication in carburettor design and are leading us into the era of injection. For racing, this has been the case for the past ten years.

Inlet ports and valves

The transition of the manifold from carburettor or injection air control body to the port and valve should be as a gradually reducing cross-sectional area to ensure that maximum efficient gas velocity is achieved. This is around 400ft/sec. and this should be reached as close to the valve as possible. In the case of the four-stroke, this will be just upstream of the valve guide boss where the port must start opening out to reduce velocities in the throat and around the valve head. For the two-stroke, maximum velocity can occur at the piston skirt face.

When we refer to valves, we mean of course the poppet valve in the four-stroke engine as opposed to the sleeve valve (long ago discarded in four-stroke engines) retained by the 2-stroke in the form of the piston skirt covering and uncovering the ports. It is a pity that the efficient flow characteristics of the poppet valve are denied the two-stroke because of the difficulty of driving them at crankshaft speed. However, the facts are unavoidable: a well designed inlet port and valve (D.7) achieves a discharge coefficient of approaching 100%, whilst the sleeve valve of the two-stroke (D.8) only reaches about 80% at its most efficient. The discharge coefficient is the ratio of the amount of gas it will pass, compared to its size.

All inlet tract joints should be accurately matched, *ie* carb to manifold and manifold to port, including gaskets. Every stepped joint will cause turbulence in the stream and will sap valuable speed from the ingoing charge.

All corners should be radiused to remove potential flow interruption, but not at the cost of removing too much metal and losing the correct shape. For example, in D.9 careless removal of metal at 'A' will result in a port flow that is so bad that it would have been better left as standard. The correct modification is shown by the dotted line.

Inlet valve guide bosses can be smoothed and streamlined but the valve stem is unalterably round and will eventually control the turbulent pattern in the throat. In some ports there is a case for removing the inlet guide and boss right back to the port wall, providing there is sufficient guide length left to fully support the valve and hold it square on the seat. Areas adjacent to the inlet valve seat should be radiused to create a blend from port wall to valve seat and from seat to combustion chamber roof. Careful attention in this area alone can raise the flow coefficient by over 10%. Similarly, the shape of the valve head is of great importance and, although true individual valve head shapes can only be determined by knowing the characteristic of the port, as a general rule of thumb, 'flat' ports as used in BMC A-series engines work best with 'penny on a stick' valve heads, while downdraught ports give best flow with a 'tulip' or spherically backed valve head.

16

D9. 4-stroke inlet port modifications.

36. Piston-valved racing Yamaha.

37. 2-stroke, piston valved, motocrosser: Suzuki RM80.

38. Disc-valved Kawasaki 2-stroke racing KH250.

Two-stroke piston skirts can be re-worked to ensure that they fully clear the top of the port and if it has any downdraughting they should be chamfered to match. Although the sharp edges can be broken to assist flow at small openings, radiusing should not be carried out because this will make the port timing unstable.

Inlet valve timing (four-stroke)

Average production engine timing is between 240 and 260 degrees in duration with opening points varying from 5 degrees to 25 degrees before T.D.C. and closing from 40 degrees to 55 degrees after B.D.C.

Valve lifts range from 0.28in. for a 250cc cylinder to 0.4in. for a 500cc cylinder. These engines will be giving about 50 Brake Horse Power per Litre (B.H.P./L) and produce maximum power between 5500 and 6000rpm.

If we increase the level of tune in 'stages', then these characteristics will alter as indicated in the chart.

Stage	Application	Inlet V. Timing		Valve lift (in)		Potential
		BTDC	ABDC	250 cyl	500 cyl	BHP/L
Std.	Std. Saloon	20	50	0.28	0.40	50
St.1	Improved Street	30	60	0.31	0.42	62
St.2	Rally, M/Cross, Grasstrack	40	70	0.35	0.44	80
St.3	Race 1	50	80	0.35	0.44	95
	Race 2	58	88	0.40	0.48	105
SPL	Super/ch. Drag	62	92	0.40	0.50	150
SPL	Turbo/ch. Race	45	85	0.41	0.50	150

Two-stroke port timing

Because the piston uncovers the ports equally on its up and down strokes, it has symmetrical timing unless disc or other forms of rotary valve timing control are added. These methods of control invariably increase cost and complexity of the engine. It is a pity because the two-stroke does respond to asymmetric changes in inlet timing.

Whilst, in general, slight changes in inlet opening do not give power improvements, the same changes in inlet closing certainly do. Therefore, while it is necessary to lengthen inlet timing to increase power and rpm, the low speed power losses are enormous, hence the need for a lot of gear ratios. This can be offset a bit by the use of reed valves in the piston ported engine but whilst they increase low and mid-range power they lose a certain amount of top end power due to the flow restriction and the fact that, even though the reed is very light, it still has inertia which has to be overcome by the inlet stream. This in turn means that the small amount of energy required to move the reed must be taken from the inlet stream and therefore it loses a bit of high speed ram.

Previous reference has been made to the fact that the loop/scavenge or conventional crankcase induction two-stroke, is really a supercharged engine because it *sucks* the gas into the crankcase and then *blows* it into the combustion chamber. Why, therefore, doesn't it produce as much power as an externally supercharged engine? The reason is that the petrol/air mixture is fouled, either by its own intrinsic oil content or by injected hot oil being sprayed around in the crankcase.

It is also pre-heated by thermal transfer, from the surrounding hot components, further heated by compression through the transfer ports before being subjected to combustion. All this means that the combustion process is not as efficient as a four-stroke but as it happens more often it can still produce good power. Approximate changes in staged tuning of the inlet are shown in the table.

Application	Inlet Open BTDC	Duration Close ATDC	RPM at Max. Power	Potential BHP/L
Std. Street	70	70	7000	80-90
Stage 1	78	78	8500	100-120
Stage 2	90	90	12000	150-250

The choice between piston-valved and disc-valved two-stroke racing engines is still in the balance and successful machinery is divided into both categories.

The successful Yamahas (see P.36) stay with the piston valve as do most of the Motocross bikes (see P.37), but the latter tend to combine reed valves as well. On the other hand the RG500 Suzuki and Kawasaki in-line twins (see P.38) get their results using rotary valves.

Camshaft choice

The camshaft is undoubtedly the most important single component to be selected when tuning the four-stroke engine.

The correct choice is often difficult to make and this chapter is principally concerned in setting out the problems and facts, in order that the correct decision can be made for an individual application.

Recognition of the profile

The cam lobe is made up of four essential elements (see D.10). The base circle or clearance circle, often called the heel, together with the ramp — the flank — and the nose.

The base circle is the area of the cam in which little or no contact takes place with cam follower. The centre of base circle duration lies at approximately 180° from the nose centre line and is the point at which valve clearances are normally set. The ramp is the area joining base circle to flank and is designed to take up valve clearance in a controlled manner, immediately prior to the start of valve lift. The flank lifts the valve train with the spring in compression and accelerates it to its maximum speed.

The nose takes over at this point and controls the valve train deceleration until it momentarily comes to rest at full lift, when the process reverses itself to lower the valve back to its seat, where the ramp will re-open the clearance.

The whole procedure exerts an enormous strain on the components involved, sometimes 'stacking-up' contact stresses over the cam nose as high as 200,000lbs/sq.in. and calling for a high degree of accuracy in design and manufacture, together with the need for great care and attention when fitting.

Camshafts are made from either cast-iron or steel with the latter usually recognisable by their smooth forged or turned finish between the lobes as opposed to the rougher finish of the former which are left 'as cast' in this area.

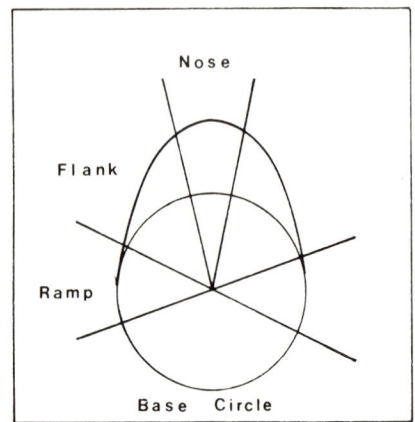

D10. Cam lobe features.

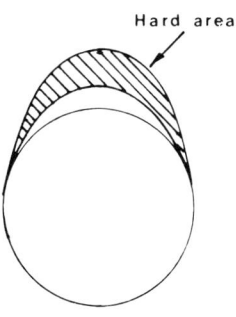

D11. Cam lobe hardness pattern (induction).

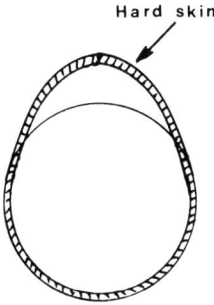

D12. Cam lobe hardness pattern (case).

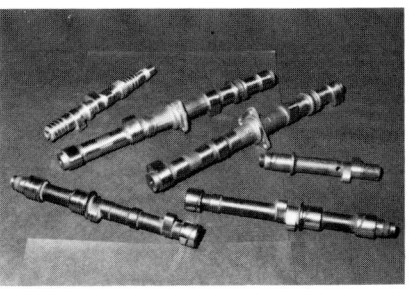

39. Motorcycle camshafts: Norton, Kawasaki and Triumph.

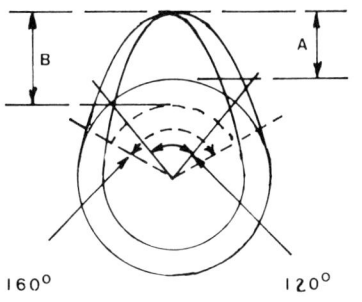

D13. Standard cam lobe with regrind profile superimposed.

In some cases they are also turned between the lobes to reduce the core size, usually done when an increase in lift dictates a smaller base circle diameter. Cast iron shafts made of 'proferal' or 'K' iron, have the lobes and gears heat treated by flame hardening or induction hardening processes, whereas 'chill cast' shafts are hardened in the vital areas during the casting process.

Whatever production method is used, cast-iron cam lobes finish up with a hardness pattern as seen in D.11, that is, about a quarter of an inch depth of hardness over the nose, tapering off down each flank. This means that the base circle is usually relatively soft, which is acceptable because there is little or no load at this point.

Because of this hardness pattern, these cams are particularly suitable for regrinding, only requiring final refinishing with the black, oil retaining, phosphate coating.

Steel cams, on the other hand, are case hardened, which means that they finish up with a thin hardened layer, usually about 0.040in. thick, which is cut through when the cam is reground. This necessitates heat treatment or hard-facing to regain acceptable hardness after a regrind.

Lobe hardness over the nose should be 50-53 Rockwell 'C' on cast-iron and 54-58 Rockwell 'C' on steel.

Camshaft regrinding — does it work?

By far the majority of European high performance camshafts are produced by the process of re-profiling the standard cam. Contrary to the misconceived opinion held by some, this procedure, if properly engineered, results in a product that is equal, both in reliability and performance, to the same component made from a raw billet.

Although it would be ideal to make all camshafts from new billets to avoid the transportation problems of exchange units, this is just not practical in Europe, due to the vast variety of makes and models, often coupled with the non-availability of unmachined castings from the original manufacturers and the obvious poor economics of producing special castings to meet the small demand for one particular model.

This situation doesn't apply in the United States where a relatively small number of billets cover a very wide range of vehicles.

To many people the process of regrinding a camshaft is a black art, resulting in the inevitable question: "How can you machine metal away from a cam and yet have it finish up with more lift?" It works like this. If we look at D.13, the hard line represents the original lobe shape and the cam lift is represented as dimension 'A', the difference between the base circle and the nose. The duration of lift is shown as 120° at the cam, which would be 240° at the crankshaft, because the camshaft rotates at half crank speed. The dotted line shows the cam shape after it has been reground and it can be clearly seen that the lift has now been increased to the dimension 'B', this time the difference between the new base circle and the nose. At the same time the duration has been increased to 160° at the cam, that is 320° at the crankshaft.

From this diagram it is also now possible to see why the cast iron cam lends itself so readily to regrinding. The deep hardness pattern over the nose is still fully effective.

Is it possible to determine the use of a cam by its shape?

The fast answer to this question is 'no'! The shape of the lobe is entirely dependent on the individual components that work with it and will vary a lot from engine to engine. This is clearly illustrated in P.40 which shows a selection of standard and racing cam shapes from a variety of engines. 'A' is a standard Fiat, 'B' is racing Jaguar, 'C' is racing Imp, 'D' is standard Triumph Bonneville, 'E' is standard Harley Davidson and 'F' is racing Honda.

It has long been the general impression that it is possible to look at a cam shape and say whether it's for road or track. P.40 shows just how inaccurate that statement can be. The ultimate example is shown in P.41, which most 'experts' would define as a very mild looking cam. In fact it's the profile used by Formula Three racing engines from 1976 onwards.

Camshaft position and drive

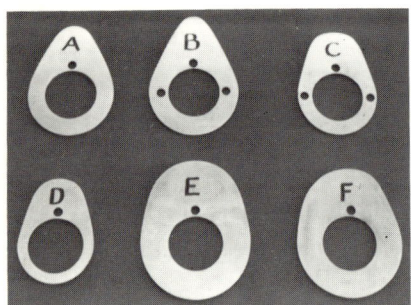

40. Camshaft lobe profiles. Note wide variation of shapes.

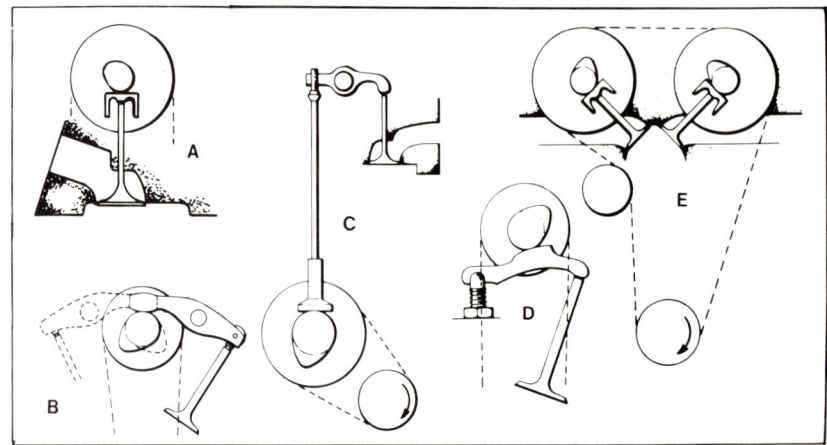

D14. Different forms of valve train in common use.

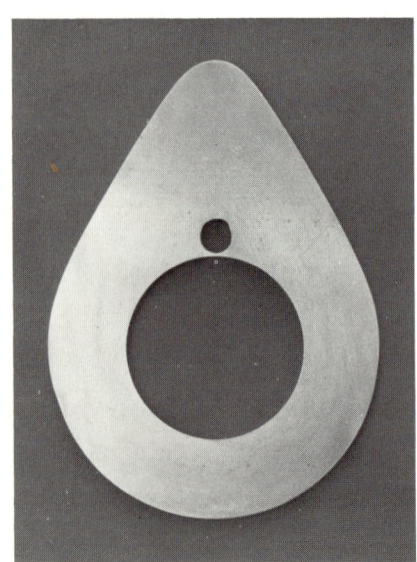

41. F3 race camshaft profile.

D.14 shows the camshaft and associated valve train component layouts covering 95% of modern engine designs.

Their applications, virtues and disadvantages are listed in the table below:

Key	Used by:	Virtues	Disadvantages
(A) S.O.H.C. Direct operating.	Chrysler, Audi, BL, Saab, Volvo, Honda, Many others.	Single camshaft simple drive, belt or chain.	Valve size restriction due to in-line layout. Bore size controls sum of inlet and exhaust seat diameters. Ports often too long.
(B) S.O.H.C. With rockers.	B.M.W., Mazda, Colt, Moskvich, BL, Peugeot, Porsche Toyota, Honda, Yamaha, Ural.	Allows better valve placing. Still simple drive.	Spark plugs position is restricted due to rockers and shafts.
(C) O.H.V. Pushrod.	Almost all car and bike manufacturers.	Ease of servicing.	Flexibility and weight of a long train of components.
(D) S.O.H.C. Loose follower finger	Datsun, Fiat Ford, Lada, Mercedes.	Ease of servicing. Choice of valve position.	Flexible by normal O.H.C. standards. Excessive overall height.

| (E) Twin cam. Direct operating. | Alfa Romeo, Aston Martin, Ferrari, Honda, Lancia Lotus, Maserati, Jaguar, Toyota, Suzuki, Kawasaki, Many others. | The only true racing layout. Allows freedom of valve and plug position. | Costly to manufacture. Difficult to service. |

Camshaft installation

As stated earlier, the camshaft is the most highly stressed component in the engine and therefore requires particular care when being fitted.

The majority of cast-iron cams have a black phosphate coating. The purpose of this is not, as many people think, a surface hardening process but it is for oil retention during the early life of the cam. It carries out this function admirably but unfortunately also retains any dirt that is brought into contact. Even just handling a camshaft with grubby hands while fitting, can implant enough tiny particles of grit to seriously shorten its life.

The rules of successful camshaft installation

Research indicates that most cams that wear out start to fail during the first few moments of operation. Many cams are irreparably damaged, even before the engine is started, because the basic rules of camshaft break-in have not been followed.

The cause of premature cam and tappet failure is metal to metal contact between the tappet and cam lobe. Should this contact occur due to lack of proper lubrication or excessively high pressure due to valve train interference shearing the oil film, then 'galling' will take place. When this happens, metal is transferred from the tappet to the cam or vice versa in a process comparable to welding. Microscopic high spots, which are present on all machined parts, become overheated due to friction and pressure and bond together, tearing sections loose from the tappet or lobe. These pieces of metal remain attached and create further local overheating during the following revolutions of the camshaft and lead to ultimate failure of the affected components. Listed below are the mistakes that lead to premature failure:

1. Inadequate lubrication during the initial rotation of the camshaft with full spring load applied.

2. Interference in the valve train due to improper installation and failure to check for interference. Valve spring coil boxing and collar guide contact or valve to valve and/or piston are the main problems.

3. Installation of used tappets with a new camshaft. No matter how good tappets look, new tappets must be used with a new camshaft!!! Beware of reclaimed tappets; they are usually ground flat whereas tappet relationships involve the use of a tapered cam lobe working with a spherically radiused tappet foot. D.15 shows an exaggerated view of this condition which essentially comprises a cam lobe taper of around 6-10 *minutes!* That's about a thou. over half an inch and a spherical radius on the tappet foot of 50-100 *inches!* The centreline of the tappet is also offset from the lobe centreline by about 0.050in.

4. Water, petrol or other contaminant in the oil that can lower film strength, or create abrasion.

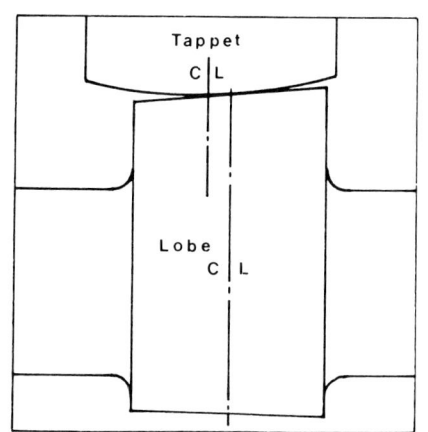

D15. The relationship of tappet base radius and cam lobe taper.

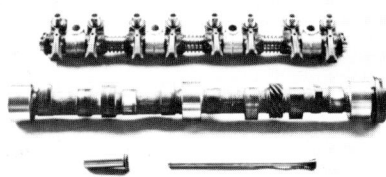

42. Camshaft, rocker assembly, pushrod and cam follower.

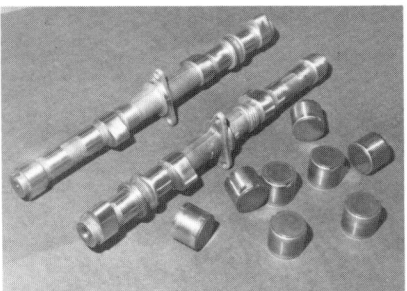

43. Camshafts and 'bucket' tappets. Note adjustment shims in top of tappets.

44. Ford ohc rocker arm/cam follower.

45. Timing disc on crank. Dial gauge on valve (Honda).

5. Excessively long cranking on the starter. Oil will not reach cam lobes until engine is running.

6. Low idle speeds during break-in. Cam lobes in pushrod engines usually depend on oil thrown from con-rods for lubrication. Oil delivery will not be sufficient at idle.

Reliable camshaft manufacturers will themselves take several precautions:

1. Supply cam profile designs that are not overloaded or highly stressed.

2. Provide cams with the correct machined finish.

3. Phosphate or otherwise treat cams to assist oil retention.

4. Supply or recommend special oil for assembly.

The mechanic handling the installation bears the greatest responsibility for break-in of the camshaft. The following outlined steps will help ensure long and trouble-free life from the camshaft and associated components:

1. Coat the cam lobes and cam face of the tappet with lubricant. If a proprietary cam lube containing Zinc-Dio-Thio-Phosphate, like Piper Cam Lube, is not available, then an E.P. 140 or 90 Hypoid rear axle oil is the next best alternative.

2. Check entire valve train for interference before attempting to start engine.

3. Set pushrod engine valve clearances 0.003in to 0.005in smaller than specified for initial start-up.

4. Before starting all engines, prime the oil system by turning oil pump manually. Fill carburettor with petrol, fill radiator, ensure correct ignition timing. Engine must start right away and not be subjected to a long grind on the starter.

5. Do not idle engine during the first twenty minutes of operation; rpm should be kept at 2500 or above; in pushrod engines oil throw-off from the crank may not be sufficient to lubricate the cam followers. Also contact stresses at the nose of the cam are very high at low speed. Engines may be run in the shop or on the road or strip. If adjustments need to be made during the twenty minutes break-in period, shut the engine down. *DO NOT IDLE!*

If the engine is dismantled for repair, maintenance or inspection, after any running at all, it is important that the tappets be kept in order. Each tappet will be mated to a cam lobe and swapping tappets may cause failure.

Camshaft – checking and setting timing

Having selected a camshaft of suitable duration and lift from the sections on inlet and exhaust characteristics and the following chart, it is now necessary to ensure that the timing is zeroed in to the specified figures.

Guide to correct camshaft selection

Std: Average standard engine figures.

Stage 1: Normal commuting, minimal modifications to carburation and ignition.
Stage 2: ½ Rally. Vehicle used for daily restricted road work/club rallying.
Stage 3: Rally. Vehicle used mainly for club rallying, occasional pro-rally.
Stage 4: Pro-rally and Race. Saloon or similar heavy vehicles.
Stage 5: Circuit racing with lightweight vehicle.
Stage 6: Intermittent ultra-high performance (ie drag-racing).

Stage	Cylinder capacity 250cc					350cc					500cc				
	IO	IC	EO	EC	VL	IO	IC	EO	EC	VL	IO	IC	EO	EC	VL
STD OR	20 1000–6000	45	45	15	.30	20 1000–6000	45	45	15	.34	20 1000–5500	45	45	15	.39
ST.1 OR	30 2000–7000	60	60	30	.35	25 1500–7000	65	65	25	.37	25 1500–6500	65	65	25	.40
ST.2 OR	38 3000–7000	66	68	36	.38	40 2000–7000	76	76	40	.38	34 1500–7000	62	64	32	.40
ST.3 OR	35 3500–8000	73	73	35	.38	44 2500–7000	78	78	44	.40	40 2000–7000	74	74	40	.42
ST.4 OR	48 4000–8000	78	78	48	.40	48 3500–7500	78	80	46	.40	48 3000–7000	78	80	46	.44
ST.5 OR	54 5000–9000	86	86	54	.40	54 4500–8000	86	86	54	.40	54 4000–7000	86	86	54	.46
ST.6 OR	58 8000–10,000	88	88	58	.40	60 7000–9000	86	88	58	.45	60 7000–9000	90	90	60	.50

IO: Inlet opens before T.D.C., **IC**: Inlet closes after B.D.C., **EO**: Exhaust opens before B.D.C., **EC**: Exhaust closes after T.D.C., **VL**: Valve lift (inches), **OR**: Operating R.P.M. range (Generally for car engines. Small capacity multi-cylinder motorcycle engines will run to appreciably higher figures).

46. Timing disc on crank. Dial gauge on tappet (V8 Aston Martin).

47. Dial gauge on tappet.

To accurately set or check timing it will be necessary to use a protractor bolted firmly to the crank nose and a dial gauge registering motion of an appropriate valve (see P.45).

First zero the protractor at T.D.C. The most accurate way of doing this is to use a modified spark plug, with a fixed probe in place of the electrode, that stops piston motion a small amount before T.D.C. Rotating the crank slowly backwards then forwards will enable accurate zeroing between the two points at which the piston is stopped. After this, all further timing checks must be carried out in the correct direction of rotation to ensure that all valve train 'slack' is taken up in the normal way.

As an example, let's suppose that a camshaft has been selected with the following characteristics:

Inlet 40° B.T.D.C. – 72° A.B.D.C. Valve lift 0.400 in
Exhaust 76° B.B.D.C. – 36° A.T.D.C. Valve lift 0.380 in.

Method 1:
Set valve clearances to a known figure, say 0.010 in. Zero the dial gauge with the valve closed. Turn the crank slowly and watch for a reading of, say, 0.005 in of valve lift and note the protractor reading. Continue to turn the crank through the opening and closing phases of lift until the dial gauge returns to the same reading and note the protractor reading again. Repeat the procedure with the other valve and then convert the protractor readings to their appropriate 'before and after T.D.C. and B.D.C.' status.

48. Adjustment of cam timing by vernier, or hole elongations, or offset dowels.

49. Offset dowels and keys to aid cam timing adjustment.

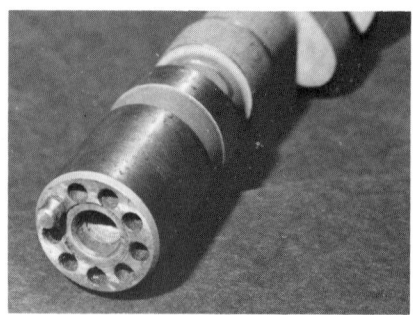

50. Vernier adjustment holes in cam.

51. Adjustment of cam timing by hole elongation.

This method is often not very satisfactory due to the fact that uncontrollable valve train movement takes place, caused by clearance or wear in rockers and shafts or tappets and guides etc., which tends to give a distorted indication of start and finish of valve motion.

Method 2:

If the valve lift at a given crank angle is known, say at T.D.C., then the timing can be set accurately by the following procedure. Install the camshaft on standard timing marks with the valve clearances set to the correct running value. Zero the dial gauge with the chosen valve on its seat. Now turn the crankshaft to T.D.C. and note the valve lift. If it is not correct then disconnect the cam drive and rotate the camshaft alone until the correct lift is achieved. Re-couple the drive using one of the methods discussed below to accommodate the need for a small amount of angular change. Twin-cam engines will need a lift figure for both inlet and exhaust valves. Always start by adjusting the shaft that comes first in the drive-line and always ensure that the drive is held at running tension while readings are being taken.

Method 3:

Valve full lift position. This is probably the most accurate method and requires that the full lift position of the inlet and/or the exhaust valve be worked out in the following way. Referring to our 'example' cam at the start, the inlet timing is:

40° B.T.D.C. – 72° A.B.D.C.

From these timing figures we can say that the total timing duration is:

40 + 180 + 72 = 292°

The full lift of the valve will occur halfway through this period, which is 292 divided by two, or 146. So, if full lift occurs 146° after the start of valve motion, and valve motion itself starts at 40° *before* T.D.C., then full lift must occur at 146 minus 40, or 106° *after* T.D.C. Similarly, the full lift position of the exhaust valve can be calculated to be 110° *before* T.D.C.

The cam timing can now be set by following the initial procedure described in 'Method 2' and then turning the crank to the appropriate position, say, in the case of the inlet, 106° A.T.D.C. At this point, the cam drive can be disconnected and the camshaft rotated slightly, until the inlet valve is fully open, at which point the drive should be reconnected.

Don't rely on eyeball judgement of the dial gauge to decide the position of full lift. Velocity in this area is so low that there is an apparent period of dwell and it would be inaccurate to try and guess the centre point of this period.

To be safe, take a point each side of the full lift, say 0.020 in. before and after, note the protractor readings at these two points, add the two together and divide by two. This will give you the true angular reading.

Having checked and corrected the timing, it will probably be necessary to use an offset dowel or key (see P.49) to couple up the drive in the correct position, although some of the more sophisticated engines are built with a vernier cam drive adjustment, which makes life a lot easier. (See P.50).

Kawasaki, Honda, Yamaha, and other centre drive cams, will have to be advanced one complete tooth and then the drive bolt holes filed out in the direction opposite in rotation until the correct position is reached. (See P.51).

52. 2-stroke inlet, with piston clearing port ready for inlet charge.

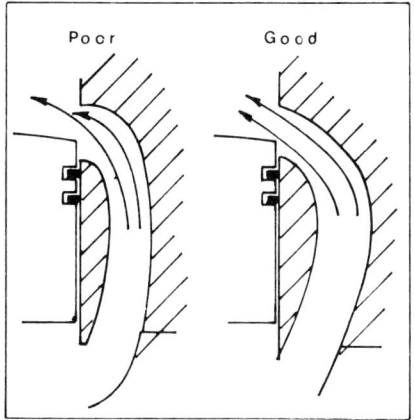

D16. 2-stroke transfer port comparison.

53. Inlet port of 2-stroke fully open with piston at B.D.C.

54. 2-stroke exhaust port, closed by piston.

Two-stroke port timing — checking and modification

Although not generally recognised, there is a close affinity between the two-stroke and four-stroke engine in many respects. The equivalent of the camshaft in the two-stroke engine, is the piston, opening and closing the valves in relation to crank rotation.

As described earlier, these are in effect sleeve valves, which do not have efficient flow capability and therefore have to be larger in relationship to a given cylinder size.

Whilst it is relatively easy to change the valve timing of a four-stroke by just changing the camshaft, it requires a lot more skill and sensitivity to efficiently change the timing of a two-stroke.

As with all engines, the first step in accurate checking is again to fit a protractor to the crank, with a firmly mounted pointer that will give an exact and repeatable indication of crank angle. It should be zeroed at T.D.C. by the piston stop method described on Page 23.

Inlet timing can be measured by looking straight into the inlet port and trapping a two thou. feeler gauge between the bottom of the piston skirt and the lower edge of the port. Take a note of the protractor reading. Rotate the crank so that the piston rises to T.D.C. and traps the feeler again as it is coming down, at which point take a further note of the angle.

Production engine timing often relies on casting and coring accuracy and can normally be considerably improved by attention to detail in the port mouth and to the respective piston skirt area.

Transfer port timing can be measured by visually checking piston motion while looking down into the cylinder. The lower lip of the port should align with the piston crown at B.D.C.

Internal modifications to the transfer are much more difficult than those to the other ports and should be carried out by experienced personnel using the right equipment. General rules are to maintain gentle port curvature. (See D.16). Any sudden changes in shape mean loss of charge energy.

Transfer timings will vary from around 75° each side of B.D.C. in road engines to about 62° each side of B.D.C. in full race units. Unlike four-stroke characteristics, increased two-stroke transfer timing duration lowers maximum power R.P.M. If the timing duration is decreased then the R.P.M. at which maximum power is produced will be higher. This is due to the fact that crankcase pressure is increased and maintained, either by the addition of a disc or reed valve, or by high speed induction ram.

However, in general, transfer timing alterations do not have a great effect on power output and provided sensible matching and smoothing is carried out, time is better spent on other tuning aspects.

Exhaust ports are relatively easy to check and rework and result in good power response.

Optimum results are usually obtained with timings of around 80° each side of B.D.C., with increases in this figure moving the power curve down the speed range, with losses in maximum power resulting from losses in trapped compression ratio.

Decreases of this figure result in an increase in maximum power, higher up the speed range, but at the expense of considerable power loss in the mid and lower speed range.

Appreciable gains can be achieved by increasing the angular width of the port, but at the same time thermal stresses in the piston ring will increase as it 'bulges' into the port mouth, so this operation must be carried out with great discretion or reliability will be lost.

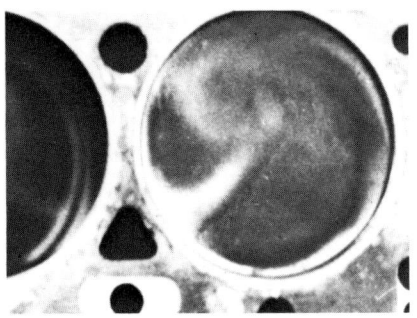

55. Carbon formation on piston showing swirl pattern of inlet charge.

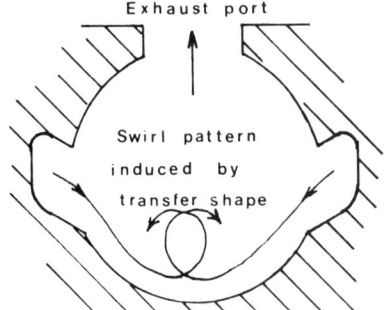

D17 2-stroke Swirl pattern.

56. 2-stroke combustion chamber with central spark plug.

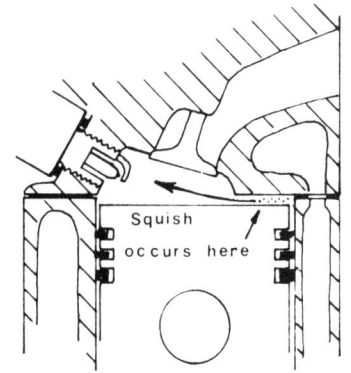

D18 The creation of Squish.

Combustion — the power stroke

Four-stroke and two-stroke characteristics re-unite during the process of combustion. In both cases, a fast efficient burn is a major key to high power output and the factors that control it are common to both.

As the piston rises, the mixture is compressed and consequently undergoes a rise in temperature. As the cylinder pressure rises to about 200 psi, which will occur somewhere between 30° and 50° *before* T.D.C., the plug fires and the combustion process starts.

Once again, it must be stressed that *IT IS A PROCESS OF BURNING — IT IS NOT AN EXPLOSION.*

An explosion is the result of uncontrolled detonation which does occur in the internal combustion engine occasionally and, if allowed to continue unchecked, produces disastrous results.

As combustion continues, the cylinder pressure rises to between 800 and 1000psi to create the driving force on the piston crown. This maximum pressure varies with engine design, but a good rule of thumb is that it will be about one hundred times the compression ratio. The efficiency with which combustion takes place is controlled by a number of important factors that readily respond to adjustment or modification and are equally applicable in both two- and four-stroke engines. They are as follows:

Swirl

Control of movement of the inlet mixture as it enters the combustion chamber, as a result of the correct shaping or reshaping of the inlet port and valve, or the transfer port. This results in a turbulent pattern within the inlet charge, which in turn creates a pre-mixing effect of the richer and weaker portions of the charge and assists even burning (see D.17 and P.55).

Combustion chamber shape and finish

A neat, minimum size combustion chamber ensures that flame-spread is a rapid process, thus permitting latest possible ignition, *ie* a minimum of spark advance (see section on ignition control, page 31).

This is one area in which the two-stroke engine really scores, because its lack of valve head intrusion in the combustion chamber means that the chamber can be of near perfect, small part spherical design, with the plug in the centre (See P.56).

Combustion chamber finish should be smooth and highly polished to reflect heat back into the chamber and to retard the build-up of carbon related deposits which can cause detonation or run-on. Having selected the desired compression ratio, chamber volumes should be balanced to within half a cc between all cylinders.

Squish

The final compressive shock received by the charge, immediately before the start of combustion. Created by close proximity of certain areas of the piston crown to the cylinder head face at T.D.C. (See D.18). This gap can be as little as 0.030 in. or less, depending on crank and con-rod stretch at high R.P.M. and mixture in these areas is driven into the combustion chamber, closer to the ignition point.

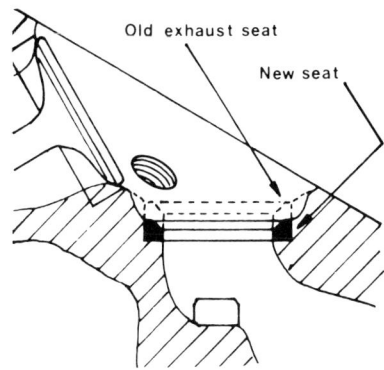

D19. Recessing of exhaust valve seat.

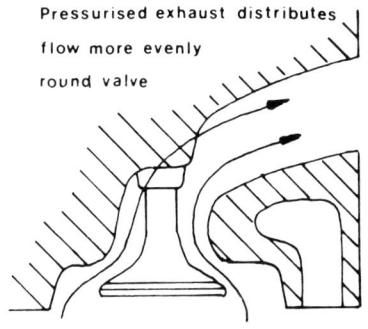

D20. Correct exhaust port shape.

57. 4-into-1 exhaust system on 4-stroke motorcycle.

58. 4-into-2-into-1 tuned 4-stroke exhaust manifold.

Compression ratio

The ratio of the swept volume of the cylinder to the compressed volume of the cylinder. Calculated as follows:

$$\text{Compression ratio} = \frac{\text{Swept volume} + \text{Clearance volume}}{\text{Clearance volume}}$$

C.R.s vary from 8 to 1, used for standard engines, up to 12 to 1 for petrol burning race engines and 15 to 1 for alcohol burning race engines.

C.R.s for two-stroke engines are often calculated using trapped volume above the exhaust port, instead of true swept volume. This means that it varies with exhaust timing and, calculated on this basis, the results are much lower and vary from 7 to 1 up to 9.5 to 1.

The exhaust system — Four-stroke

The four-stroke exhaust system consists of considerably more than the visible external manifold and pipe, and starts at the exhaust valve.

The valve itself needs to be much heavier in design at the back of the head than the inlet valve, in order to cope with the hot exhaust blast. Do not be tempted to remove any of the protruding valve guide. The valve is continuously trying to shed its heat, and relies on contact with the guide and seat for this process. For the same reason, the seat width must always be greater than for inlet valves and should be between 0.080 in. and 0.100 in., depending on cylinder and valve size.

Modifications to the exhaust port should consist of increasing the bowl area around the stem and guide, and then a smooth blend to the chosen pipe size. As far as shape is concerned, a short straight section running into an up-draughted port gives the best flow/diameter ratio (see D.20) and, just as with the inlet port, radiusing sharp corners will also improve flow.

The exhaust cam

When fitting a full-race cam, the valve lift at T.D.C. is considerably increased. A 400cc cylinder, in standard trim, will have about 0.080 in. of lift at overlap T.D.C. When a full-race cam is fitted, this will increase to around 0.200 in. This happens to both inlet and exhaust valves, so valve to piston clearance and valve to valve clearance is reduced considerably.

One way to alleviate this problem is to pocket the exhaust valve head as seen in D.19. Unlike the inlet, the flow capability of the exhaust actually improves with partial masking. This presents us with the convenient option of recessing the exhaust valve to improve clearance.

Exhaust pipe length and size

As the exhaust valve opens, a pressure wave front is created which travels down the exhaust pipe at the speed of sound. As this pressure wave reaches the end of the pipe, it expands and a negative or suction pulse travels back up the pipe towards the engine. As it reaches the cylinder, it reverses again and moves back towards the end of the pipe.

This fluctuating pressure pulse effect can be used to great advantage in tuning the engine. If the system is designed in such a way that the negative or suction pulses return to the cylinder at overlap T.D.C., then they will assist in clearing the combustion chamber of exhaust gases. In turn, this will cause a depression at the inlet valve which will help draw in the inlet charge. Coupling the pipes of multi-cylinder engines will also mean that the pulse effects from

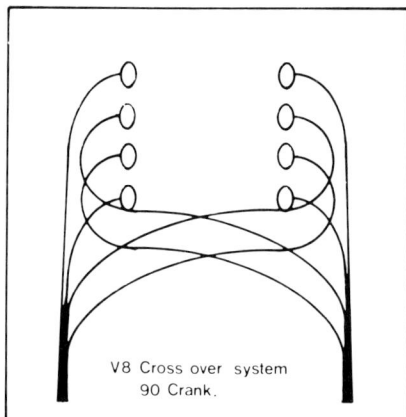

D21. V8 cross-over exhaust pattern.

59. Open stub exhaust on drag racing car.

60. Exhaust system detail on F1 McLaren.

one cylinder can be used to assist the breathing of another. The following formula can be used to calculate the ideal length for a given application:

$$L = \frac{5100 \times E.T.}{R.P.M. \times 6}$$

Where:
- L = Primary pipe length in inches measured from the exhaust valve head.
- E.T. = Exhaust valve duration in degrees from point of opening to T.D.C.
- R.P.M. = The estimated revs, at which max. power will be achieved minus five hundred.

Example: If the exhaust timing is 80° B.B.D.C. to 50° A.T.D.C. and the estimated maximum power R.P.M. is 7200, then E.T. will be 80 + 180 = 260, and R.P.M. will be 7200 − 500 = 6700.

Having calculated the primary pipe length, we must now calculate the diameter as follows.

Take the cylinder capacity in ccs and double it.
Divide this by 16.4 to bring it to cubic inches.
Divide by 'L' as previously calculated.
Divide by 3.14.
Find the square root.
Multiply by two and add 0.120.

This will give the O.D. of the tube in inches which, at first sight, will appear rather small. This is because it assumes a perfectly smooth straight pipe, which is impractical to use, so the following allowances must be made.

To allow for the viscous drag created in the bends used in an 'average' primary pipe and also to allow for the slight pipe flattening that takes place at the bends, increase the internal cross-sectional area by 10-15%. This will probably finish up as a pipe size that is non-standard, so go for the nearest available diameter *above* this figure.

Remember that 'L' is from the exhaust valve head, so the exhaust port length will have to be deducted to get the actual manufacturing length. This will then give the joining point of the primary pipes.

From this point, the secondary or tailpipe length can be 'L' or any multiple of 'L' and its diameter can be calculated using the method above, but by starting off with four times the cylinder capacity for a four cylinder engine, or three times for a 'six'.

'Fours' should always finish up in a single tailpipe, while 'sixes' should finish up with twin pipes, one of which couples cylinder numbers 1, 2 and 3 and the other coupling cylinder numbers 4, 5 and 6.

Production V8s with 90° cranks should ideally have a cross-over system as seen in D.21, but this is usually impractical, in which case they can be treated as two 'fours', but will need a balance pipe linking the tailpipes at a tuned length. Racing V8s with 180° cranks can be correctly treated as two 'fours' with no balance pipe necessary.

If a silencer is used, expansion will take place, so the start of the chamber should occur at a 'tuned' tailpipe length, with additional tailpipe added to clear exhaust gas as necessary.

This chart is only intended as a guide. Individual engine applications will vary with engine characteristics and slight changes will be needed to achieve maximum performance. Cam timings for turbocharged and supercharged engines are dealt with in the relevant section.

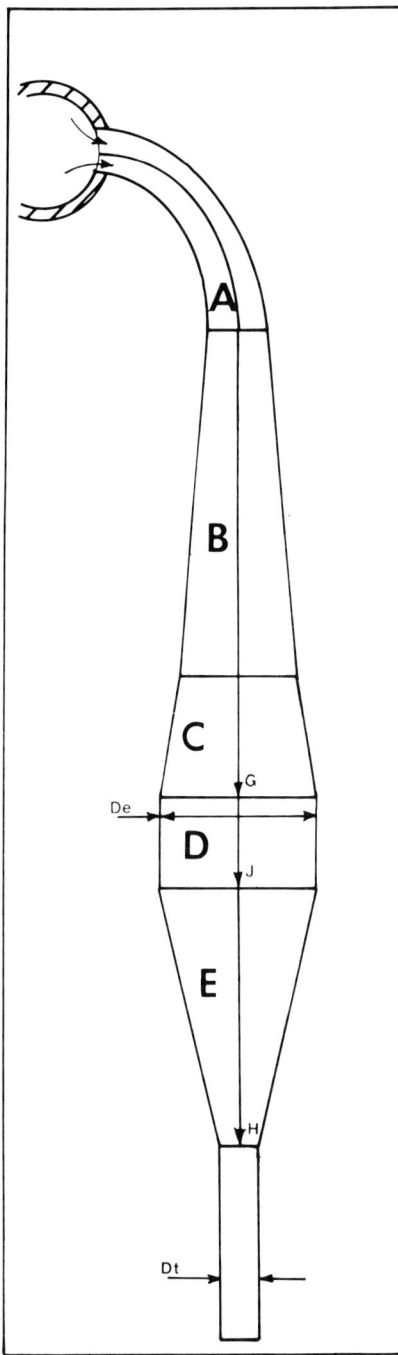

D22. Tuned 2-stroke exhaust.

61. Suzuki 2-stroke race bike with tuned exhaust system.

Exhaust timing selection chart

Application	Exhaust opens B.B.D.C.	Exhaust closes A.T.D.C.	Av. max. power R.P.M.	E.T.
Standard Engine	50°	20°	5500	230
Stage 1 Street	65°	30°	6200	245
Stage 2 Rally, M/Cross	75-80°	40-50°	6800	260
Stage 3 Advanced Rally and M/Cross	82°	54°	7400	262
Stage 4 Full Circuit Race	88°	56°	8000+	268
Dragster	90°+	60°+	8000+	270+

The exhaust system — Two-stroke

The pressure pulse reversal as described earlier also takes place in the two-stroke exhaust system and can be used to much greater effect if correctly manipulated due to the fact that the whole breathing process is dependent on a transfer of pressure from one area to another and is not positively valve controlled as it is in the four-stroke. The rules of good design are not nearly as easy to lay down and best results are ultimately only achieved by exhaustive dynamometer testing. Even then the results obtained will not apply to another engine if there is any slight variation in timing. Multi-cylinder coupling is not mathematically feasible except in three cylinder configurations and even then, the improvement comes in the mid-range. Ultimate power from multi-cylinder engines demands that they be treated as a group of single cylinders. This often creates great difficulty in accommodating the mass of snake-like hardware as can be witnessed in P.61.

The basic components of the exhaust system are laid out in D.22, and they function in the following manner:

(A) Primary Pipe
Often a parallel tube, particularly in production road machines; the ideal is a tapered primary pipe to control the expansion rate of the high speed gas slug ejected from the port and convert its kinetic energy into pressure energy.

(B) Primary Divergent Cone
Controls initial expansion of the pressure pulse and is often combined with:

(C) Secondary Divergent Cone
Which finally controls the pressure pulse expansion to induce the negative pulse which travels back to the port to help scavenge the cylinder.

(D) Expansion Chamber
Length acts as a time control before throttling of the gas slug which starts at:

(E) Convergent Cone
Which throttles down the slug to the:

(F) Tail Pipe
The size of which controls the high pressure reverse 'plug', which in turn pushes the overspill of intake charge back into the cylinder before the piston shuts the door.

The whole sequence, using correctly designed components, will result in a cylinder filling efficiency of more than 100% at the 'tuned' engine speed.

True design formulae for these systems are highly complex and still not quite fully understood, but outlined below is a simplified starting point for those who want to have a go themselves:

$$\text{Length 'G' in inches} = \frac{1650 \times TD}{R.P.M.}$$

Where TD is transfer port duration in degrees.
R.P.M is desired 'on pipe' R.P.M.

$$\text{Length 'H' in inches} = \frac{1650 \times ED}{R.P.M.}$$

Where 'ED' is exhaust port duration in degrees.

$$\text{Length 'J' in inches} = \frac{1650 \times (TD + C)}{R.P.M.}$$

Where 'C' will control the length of the parallel section and lengthen time before reverse plug starts. Find empirically by starting at 0° and increasing in 5° intervals.

'De' will be around 2.25 x Piston diameter for high revs and 2.0 x Piston diameter for torque.

'Dt' will be around 0.45 x Piston diameter for high revs and 0.5 x Piston diameter for torque.

Chapter 3
Ignition

Whether for car or motorcycle, two-stroke or four-stroke, the need for an ignition system is universal and the operating principles of all of them are the same. Only the components used to do the job vary in design.

All types of system need to use a coil, either readily identifiable as the cylindrical object with the H.T. cable leading to distributor and spark plugs, or not so obvious as an integrated part of the magneto or mag-flywheel.

The coil consists of two windings and an iron core that can be magnetised. Current is fed into the primary winding and then interrupted. When this interruption takes place, a high voltage is induced in the secondary winding which discharges itself via the spark plugs.

The method of feeding current to the primary can either be from a battery, which is part of a continuously re-charging electrical system as used on a car or bike larger than about 150cc, or it can be direct from a generator that is integral with the magneto or flywheel.

Interruption of the primary current is a switching operation which is carried out mechanically by a contact-breaker, or electronically, using transistors. At this stage, some method of ignition timing variation is also introduced to advance the spark as engine rpm increases. This is also the stage at which we must start giving some thought to modification.

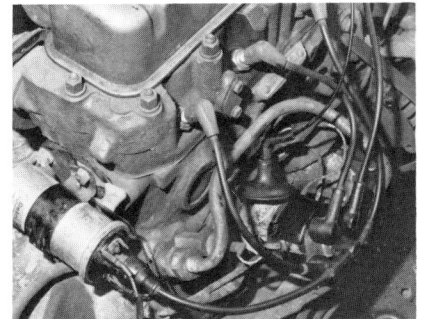

62. Coil, distributor and plug leads (Road car).

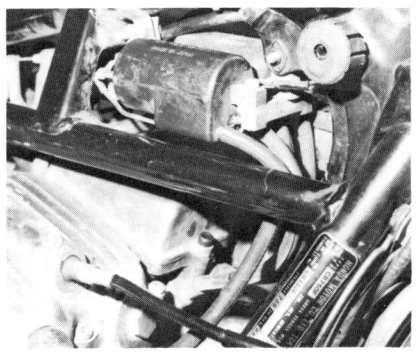

63. Motorcycle ignition (multiple coils).

64. Four-stroke contact breakers (Fiat Strada).

Is ignition advance necessary?

Although the compressed mixture is highly inflammable as previously discussed, it is not explosive and therefore has to undergo a burning process that takes time, albeit only one or two milliseconds. This burn time must be taken into consideration in order to produce maximum combustion pressure just at the right time — as the piston is starting to descend. If it occurs too early it is resisting the natural motion of the moving parts and will set up alarming stresses in piston, con-rod and crankshaft. If it occurs too late, then potential driving force on the piston is wasted.

So, ignition advance is necessary to compensate for the 'burn time' between spark occurring and point of maximum pressure build-up. This burn time varies according to engine design characteristics, as explained in the section on combustion (page 26), and, measured in crankshaft degrees, is a fair guide to the combustion efficiency of the combined power producing components. Examples of these variations can be seen in the table on page 30, which compares the various ignition advance requirements of standard engines to those needed in modified form. The 850 Mini, top of the list with highest advance of 42° at relatively low rpm, indicates poor combustion and Ev (Volumetric Efficiency). The 1000 Mini needs 32° and at higher revs. Yet this has the same port sizes, compression ratio and valve lift, showing that just an increase in bore area has improved Ev and combustion by reducing valve masking. The 1275 Mini, with its big bore, big ports and valves, together with high compression ratio, takes a sharp upward jump in efficiency with combustion improving slightly more than breathing, thus allowing rpm for maximum advance to drop slightly. (See P.65).

On the other hand, the Maxi, with a change in capacity from 1500cc to 1750cc by increasing the stroke only, needs no apparent change in its advance at all. So this would indicate that bore size is a controller of ignition advance.

The Imp and Imp Sport show the effect of changing from one carb to two without altering any internals, whilst the Avenger comparison shows the effect of changing cam and valves in addition to the extra carb.

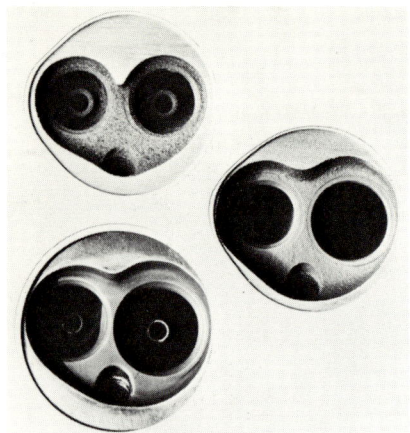

65. Mini 850, 1000, & 1250cc combustion chambers and gaskets.

66. Advance mechanism, showing springs and weights (Peugeot 305).

67. Advance mechanism, showing springs and weights (Honda 650).

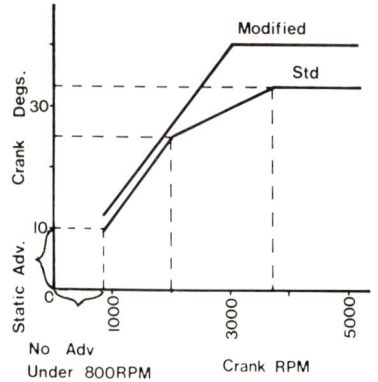

D23. Advance curve diagram.

Selecting a suitable advance curve

The Dolomite and Dolomite Sprint comparison is the best example of production engine changes showing what happens when we start modifying for ultimate performance.

The bore changes from 87 to 90mm, compression ratio from 9:1 to 9.5:1, and two valves per cylinder to four valves per cylinder. Power jumps from 68bhp. at 5200rpm to 95 at 5700rpm, yet there is only one more degree of advance needed and at much lower rpm. Why? Because the four valve layout is so much more efficient in all respects, with better breathing from the valve area and a fast burn from the central plug in a compact combustion chamber.

Make	Standard		Modified		
	Max.Adv. Degrees	RPM	Static Adv.	Total Adv.	RPM
850 Mini	42	3500	10	42	4000
1000 Mini	32	4900	10	38	4500
1275 Mini GT	30	4000	5	36	4500
1275 Mini S	27	7000	2	30	5000
1500 Maxi	35	6000	10	38	4600
1750 Maxi	35	6000	10	38	5000
875 Imp	31	5200	10	40	4500
875 Imp Sport	37	6000	12	40	5000
998 Imp	31	5000	10	46	5000
Avenger	32	4500	12	34	3500
Avenger GT	30	3000	10	38	4800
Dolomite	27	3600	8	32	3500
Dolomite Sprint	28	2100	10	32	2500
Ford Fiesta 1100	37	4700	10	38	4000
Escort 1300GT	28	4700	10	36	5200
Mexico 1600	30	4000	8	34	4000
Escort 1600BDA	25	4000	10	32	5000
Escort 2000RS	28	4500	8	36	3500
Ford 3000 V6	35	4400	10	38	3000
Jaguar 3.8/4.2	36	5400	8	40	3200
Rover 3.5 V8	30	4800	10	32	3000
Vauxhall 2300 OHC	32	3800	10	38	4000
Kawasaki 900/1000	40	3000	10	40	3000
Honda 750/1000	36	6000	10	40	3500
Norton 750 Twin	34	5000	5	38	3000
Tri/BSA Twins	36	4500	10	40	3000

'The modified' columns are based on an average tuning stage, about Stage 2, comprising multiple carbs, 9.5:1 to 10:1 C.R., valve timing with more than 70° of overlap, oversize ports and valves and multi-branch exhaust manifold. Each application will require individual adjustment but these are reasonable starting points.

Two-stroke engines will require little or no change from standard, because their near perfect, compact combustion chamber shape means that almost no flame-spread time increase takes place with modification.

Advance curves can be altered by modifying the springs and stops that control motion of the centrifugal weights, usually situated behind or under the contact-breaker housing. Typical curves of standard and modified form are shown in D.23.

68. 2-stroke contact breakers.

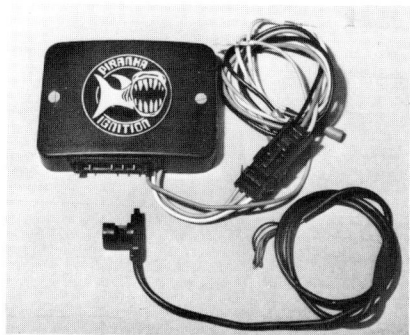
69. Piranha electronic ignition.

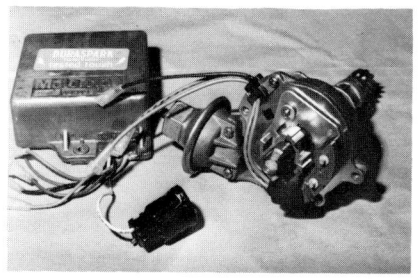
70. Electronic ignition (Ford Fiesta).

71. Flywheel ignition trigger.

Electronic ignition

Although it's done a good job for many years, the mechanical contact-breaker system is, at best, an inaccurate and unreliable method of triggering the spark. It is at its worst when running direct on the crankshaft, as used on many Japanese motorcycles (see P.68), subjected to the lateral movement and vibrations that are part of the crankshaft's natural operation. Stroboscopic observation and accurate timing checks at high speed show it to be far worse than the conventional distributor.

Modern technology has presented us with the means of switching the primary coil current electronically by 'transistorised ignition', now proven to be accurate and reliable. All the systems now available work on the same basic principles, although they may vary in detail.

Initial triggering is carried out as a result of either a magnetic, inductive, or optical signal starting a series of transistor switching functions which finish up breaking the primary coil circuit.

Apart from having the obvious advantage of no mechanical coupling, other than the rotor drive, the extremely high switching time means that the coil has much longer to recover and consequently delivers high H.T. voltages. This means higher spark energy and better combustion.

Don't be misled — electronic ignition is no magic power pack, a well maintained contact-breaker system is still good to 7000rpm plus, but it will disappear in the very near future.

Ideal small two-stroke ignition comes from the electronic flywheel (P.72) which combines power generator, transistor switching and electronic advance curve, in one neat solid state pack.

Although we said earlier how undesirable it is to have contact-breaker mechanisms running direct on the crankshaft, the true ignition relationship is between crank and spark plug, therefore the ideal trigger should be at the crank.

The best way of doing this is shown in P.71 where the ignition is triggered from the flywheel rim. Obviously, the bigger diameter that we can work at, the higher the degree of accuracy.

Spark plugs — selection and mixture checking

Having made the choice between mechanical and electronic systems, the remainder of the ignition system will give great rewards for careful attention to detail.

The spark plug handles the hot end of the ignition chain and should be selected and treated with care.

It functions by converting a small mass of compressed air into electrified particles or 'ions', thus exciting a spark to jump the gap. Running temperature should lie between 400°C and 955°C. If spark plugs are colder than this, they will foul up and, if hotter, will overheat and cause pre-ignition.

It should be made clear at this point that, although plug colouring can be used to confirm that a correct mixture is being used, mixture itself should never influence plug choice.

Correct plug choice is influenced by the compression ratio, spark advance and power output of an individual engine design and can only finally be determined as a result of dynamometer tests. It is often very difficult to make this choice without these facilities, in which case it is safest to fall back on the advice of those with specialised experience, rather than have an overcooked plug nose drop through the middle of a piston.

72. Magnetic trigger for electronic ignition.

73. Toyota on full load (full throttle, uphill).

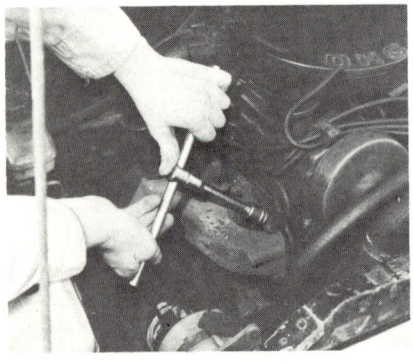

74. Removing a spark plug.

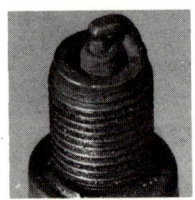 

75 & 76. Sooted spark plug (left). Normal spark plug (right).

Having made the right plug selection, the best way to check for correct mixture is as follows. Choose a long hill that will hold your top speed to, say, 60mph at full throttle. Hold full throttle for as long as possible, then flick into neutral and switch off the ignition — mind you don't lock the steering!! Remove plugs and check visually, the side electrode should be faintly blue and the insulator should be milk chocolate colour. No soot or excessive white deposits should be visible.

If the plug is running too hot, the side electrode will be burned black and the insulator will be chalk white, so having ensured that it is the recommended grade, richen the mixture until the colour is O.K.

If the mixture is too rich, the plug will be matt black on the side electrode and around the rim with a dark brown to black colouring on the insulator.

If pre-ignition or detonation has occurred, fine silver beads will probably be seen around the insulator.

Spark intensity depends on good, sharp-edged electrodes and gaps as small as can be reasonably used. Average gaps can be reduced to 0.020 in., but racing plugs will run as small as 0.016 in.

H.T. leads should ideally be of the wire cored variety, but are not essential and self-suppressed lead in *good condition* can be adequate.

The real key to a successful ignition system is high voltage, which depends on the correct selection and treatment of all the components involved.

Ignition of the near future will be entirely electronically controlled, with sensors detecting engine requirement all the time and feeding data back to a microprocessor which will, in turn, adjust the ignition advance to suit.

Combustion will be initiated by a system such as 'Plasma Jet', a high energy form of ignition, which ionises the compressed air in a cavity within the plug body and then shoots a jet of flame an inch or more into the combustion chamber, resulting in faster flame-spread and a drastic reduction in ignition advance requirement.

Later on, and possibly the ultimate ignition method, will be some form of 'Laser Igniter'.

Chapter 4
Turbocharger or Supercharger?

Turbocharger or Supercharger?

The turbocharger and supercharger both perform the function of ramming in the inlet charge rather than allowing it to be naturally induced. They vary somewhat in their method of operation and both have inherent advantages and disadvantages.

If we look at the power 'pie' diagram in D.24, it will be seen that, of every 100% of heat energy put in, in the form of fuel, only 15-30% actually gets converted into usable horsepower, whereas nearly 40% gets dumped as waste heat, down the exhaust pipe. The turbocharger uses this energy to drive a turbine coupled to and driving a centrifugal compressor. This in turn, takes the inlet air, or in some cases the inlet mixture, if the carburettor is upstream, and rapidly accelerates it, causing adiabatic compression in the inlet manifold. As the inlet valve opens, this pressure drives inlet gas into the combustion chamber. The component can be clearly seen in P.77. A schematic of the way in which it is united with the engine can be seen in D.25. The rotors of turbines and compressors of this type need to spin at very high speeds, with a maximum in excess of 100,000rpm. Obviously, this calls for a high degree of precision in manufacture and servicing.

Supercharging compressors (see D.26) which take the form or a 'Roots' or 'Vane' pump (see D.27) use a positive drive from the crankshaft. In fact, these are not true compressors but are positive displacement pumps which pack in 'slugs' of gas faster than the engine can digest them. Both types carry the gas round between the rotor segments and the casing and force it out opposite the intake. This type of supercharger demands a considerable amount of power to drive it. For example, the supercharger of a 1000 horsepower dragster will be consuming something in excess of 200bhp to drive it.

At first sight of these operating requirements, it would seem that the obvious choice must be the turbo, which apparently offers us something for nothing in terms of power boost. However, it's not quite as simple as that!

Because the turbo compressor accelerates according to exhaust flow, the boost at low rpm is non-existent and a properly matched turbo will really only work efficiently between mid-range and top rpm. At low speed, there can be a momentary but unpleasant lack of response as the rotors accelerate. This phenomenon will always be there until the multi-stage turbocharger is evolved, or a method of 'secondary combustion' in the exhaust manifold is used to keep the turbine spinning.

The turbocharger system of operation is fine for engines that spend most of their time in 'steady state' running like long distance trucks, 'indy' cars and power boats, but isn't really acceptable for dragsters that need to come off the line like a rocket, or for circuit racers that constantly need to be changing gear for corners. Certainly, dragsters need the instant response that is available from the supercharger at the moment of dropping the clutch.

Many people think that a way round this is to raise the engine revs high before the start, in order to start the turbo rotors spinning. But this is not so. The turbo depends on waste heat energy from an engine *on load,* to work properly. Therefore, the waste energy to drive the turbo is never there until the engine is working hard, *ie* already accelerating the vehicle.

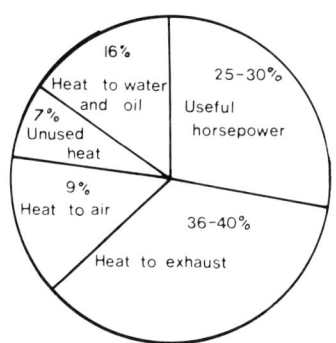

D24. Power 'pie'

77. Turbocharger unit.

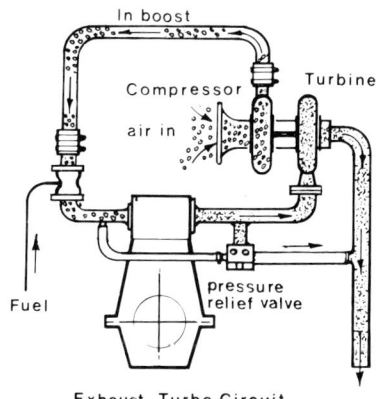

D25. Turbocharger operation.

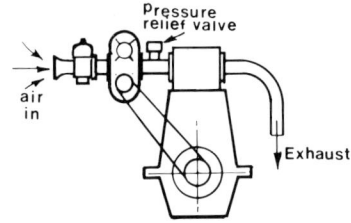

D26. Supercharger operation.

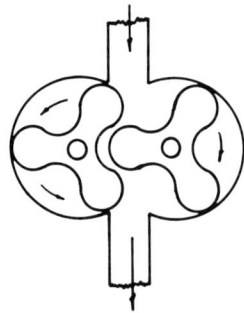

D27a. 'Roots' (lobe) type supercharging compressor.

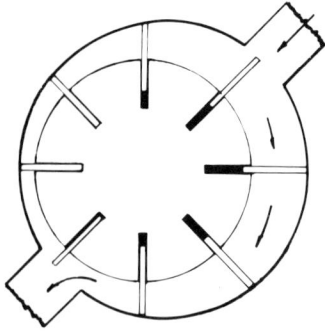

D27b. Vane type supercharging compressor.

78. Turbocharger fitted to drag bike.

Fitting a Turbocharger/Supercharger

Having made the decision which type of blower to use, the next step is to decide how to modify the engine to accept the change in power and still remain reliable.

It is possible to just bolt a kit on to a standard engine and get a good power boost, but it will only be a matter of time before some kind of mechanical disaster occurs. Bitter experience has shown that there is only one way to do it, *properly!* Strip the engine down and start from scratch! It will be cheaper in the long run ....

First consideration is space. Modern vehicles, whether cars or bikes, have already got quite a lot of hardware packed into the engine compartment.

Positive drive blowers will need a tooth-belt drive of considerable width, inevitably driving from the crank nose to keep the speed up. This alone can take up a lot of space, that could mean moving a radiator or accepting a reduction in cornering clearance on a bike. This makes the turbo drive look more attractive, but remember that turbine rotation depends on a tightly sealed exhaust system between engine and turbo. As the blower will almost certainly call for a different exhaust manifold to facilitate reasonable packaging, then the manufacture of the manifold itself becomes quite a problem. Ideally, it should be cast-iron, with heavy flat attachment faces that will guarantee a good seal. O.K. for mass production, but not for one-offs, so it must be fabricated from heavy gauge steel tube and plate to be effective. A 16-gauge manifold, with buckled and leaking faces, will kill the whole job.

The turbocharger will automatically be sited on the exhaust side of the engine, so on crossflow engines this means that the compressed inlet gas will have to be piped, either over the top of the rocker box, or round the end of the engine, to reach the inlet ports. If the carburettor is upstream of the blower, then modified throttle linkage and air cleaner must be considered. If downstream then float chamber fuel and air pressure compensating devices must be used, with all the attendant additional plumbing.

Both types of blower need additional external lubrication supply and return. This feature is critical for the turbo, with its high rotor speed, and a clear, efficient, drainback is essential to ensure that oil superheating does not take place in the bearing housing.

The oil supply should be tapped off the main gallery, then line filtered if possible, and restricted to a minimum hot flow of 0.5 galls/min. at about 30psi. Drain-back should be possible, venting into the engine above normal oil level, and with a small baffle if possible. *NO!* The dipstick hole is *not* large enough!

Both types of system will also need to incorporate some form of booster pressure control that will relieve either inlet pressure, exhaust pressure, or a combination of both.

For really high power boosting systems, an inter-cooler will also be necessary to lower the pressurised inlet gas temperature.

Engine modifications for Turbocharging/Supercharging

The first, most vital step, is to lower the compression ratio. Any reasonable final power output must depend on a boost pressure of over 10psi. A correctly matched blower, running at this figure, will give a pressure ratio in the order of 1.7:1. This means, effectively, that if you start with a C.R. of 10:1, then you

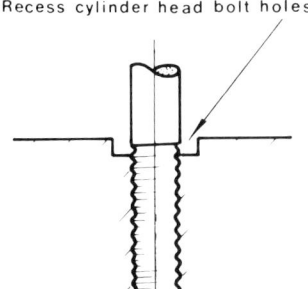

D28. *Recess at base of cyl. head bolt/stud.*

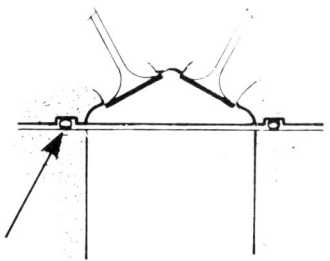

D29. *'Wills' ring seal.*

79. *Supercharged drag bike.*

80. *Turbocharged race car.*

will be running on 17:1 on full boost — a bit much for the average 98 octane fuel. Indy engines run boost pressures up to 40 and 50psi on alcohol, but petrol engines are very limited by their fuel.

However, working on the basis of 1.7:1 and assuming that an effective ratio of 13 is acceptable, then the nominal compression ratio should be lowered to: $\frac{13}{1.7} = 7.6:1$

These figures are still assuming a boost of 10psi. As boost increases the efficiency of the pumping ratio falls, so at about 30psi, which is approximately twice atmospheric pressure, the effective compression ratio is not twice the nominal, but about 1.8 x nominal.

This fortunate coincidence means that, for virtually all turbocharged or supercharged applications, the nominal or starting compression ratio should be around 7:1.

The actual process of lowering the ratio will cause more aggravation than any of the other mods. The correct way to do it is to fit low compression pistons, but unfortunately they are rarely available. This forces us into devious alternative methods:

1. Select a suitable piston from another engine, having a lower compression height, *ie* distance from gudgeon pin to crown.

2. Open up the combustion chamber in the head to a sufficient volume. This is O.K. but be careful not to overdo it and reduce wall thicknesses until they collapse under pressure.

3. Use a compression reducing plate between head and block — not advisable except as a last resort, due to the fact that the plate, usually with a head gasket on each side, acts as a heat flow barrier and will often 'cook-up' and cause detonation. If it has to be used, then the only acceptable way is sealed with 'Wills' rings, top and bottom.

With the extended cylinder pressures, head gaskets themselves can be quite a problem and must be selected and fitted with great care. Block and head surfaces must be absolutely flat and true, with not too fine a ground finish. Make sure that surfaces immediately adjacent to head stud or bolt holes are recessed to properly distribute pressure areas in head gasket.

Again, the ideal pressure seal is a 'Wills' ring, recessed into the head. (See D.29).

Camshafts for Turbocharged/ Supercharged engines

The way in which both systems produce the extra power is by extending the working pressure time on the piston. It would, therefore, seem logical to delay the exhaust opening time to take advantage of this. This is, in fact, the case with the supercharged engine and there is not much point in opening the exhaust more than about 80° B.B.D.C. However, the need to keep the turbine spinning in the turbocharger is so important that it is worth losing a little of the driving pressure and letting it out as heat energy to do this job. This means opening the exhaust up to 90° B.B.D.C., and, in fact, puts up an argument for longer exhaust timings on mild street applications to keep the turbo spinning at low engine speeds, just when it is wanted for the traffic light Grand Prix.

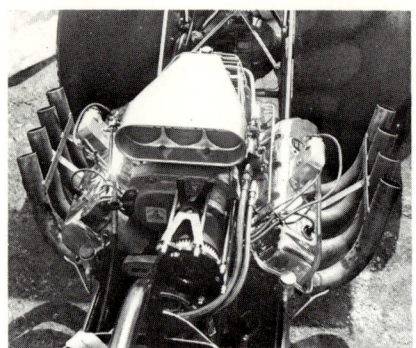

81. Supercharged dragster.

82. Dragster with airbox for supercharger.

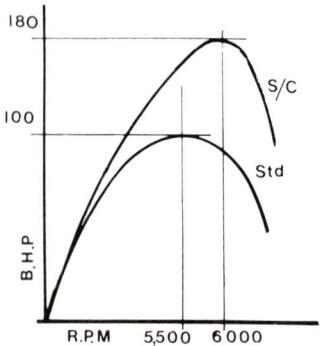

D30. Comparison of standard and supercharged power curves.

Similarly, exhaust closing times want to be slightly later for the turbo than for the supercharger, but neither of them wants to be too late or else the pressurised incoming charge will escape through the open exhaust port.

What all this comes down to is this. If you refer to page 23 you will see that average exhaust timings, whether for road or race, when worked out with method 3 of timing checks on page 24, gives exhaust valve lift positions from 100° to 110° B.T.D.C. Supercharger full lift position will lie between 110° and 115° B.T.D.C., and will effectively widen the angle between inlet and exhaust lobe centrelines.

Inlet valve timing is influenced in a slightly different way. Because the inlet charge is under pressure, the flow efficiency of the inlet valve is almost doubled and, consequently, it does not need to be open so long before T.D.C., to get good flow started. On the other hand, it is not necessary to close the inlet quite so early, because the pressure-assisted inlet flow will overcome the effect of the rising piston more readily then naturally aspirated inlet 'ram'. This will result in later than normal inlet full lift positions, which will again result in wider P.D. angles (the angle between inlet and exhaust lobe centrelines).

Although camshaft suppliers should know of these phenomena, and supply cams accordingly for turbocharged or supercharged applications, they are often not readily understood and this information will help the individual tuner to make his own choice.

The advantage of choosing the supercharger system is that it does away with many of the detailed and expensive modifications that are necessary to get a similar performance increase from a naturally aspirated engine (with the exception of ultimate race units). The power boost comes at rpm that are not much higher than standard (see D.30), which means that there are no great increases in inertia loads and that special valve springs are often not required.

Valves can remain at standard size (although it is often beneficial to increase the exhaust size) and seats can be wider. The pressure increases are in time rather than in absolute maximums and standard crank, bearings and rods, providing they are in top condition, can usually cope.

Wide power spread characteristics mean that close ratio gearboxes are unnecessary and the engine will pull high final drive ratios, to give economic road use.

The turbocharger is particularly rewarding, in that it adds the bonus of helping to clean up the exhaust and must surely be worth consideration, as a multi-stage unit fully integrated with the engine design, for future production cars and motorcycles.

Chapter 5
Engine Survival

The preceding chapters have shown how to select a group of modifications to suit individual applications and requirements.

Now they have to be built into an engine that will successfully survive the increased stresses that these modifications will impose.

There's no point in starting without mentioning the four essentials: a clean workshop, good tools, dedication and patience. Without these, you may as well forget it and hand the job over to someone else.

All assembly operations should be carried out using a thin coating of clean oil. Even check pre-assemblies need this, because even slow movement of unlubricated parts will cause minute scuffing that will, in turn, cause galling when the engine runs on power.

Valves — quality check

Check exhaust valve heads with a magnet to ensure that thay are non-magnetic austenitic, heat resisting alloy steel. British specification is 21/4N or Nimonic 80. They may be of two-piece welded construction as are many production valves, in which case the stem will be magnetic. These are O.K. for any use except full race. Inlet valves will probably be magnetic silicon chrome steel. Don't use valves with sharp cornered cotter grooves: these are potential failure points. Grooves should be semi-circular in section and the cotters should not butt face to face so that the valve can rotate, but grip the stem. Valve guides should ideally be bronze (British specification Hidural 5); cast-iron guides in good condition are O.K., but will wear quickly. Valve springs should be recommended by the cam supplier, but, anyhow, use check procedure on pages 21 and 22.

O.H.V. Engines

Check rocker gear for bush and shaft wear. Overhung end rockers should ideally be supported by additional bracketing or by using special rocker gear (see P.83). Check seating condition of spherically seated rockers of Ford V6 and Vauxhall for adequate lubrication and no signs of scuffing. (See P.84). Check pushrods for straightness and tappets for good fit in block. Fit spacers on the rocker shaft instead of springs, lighten rockers in vertical plane only (do not reduce height, only width). Lighten pushrods by slimming ends only (See D.31). Shot-peen rockers and pushrods.

Replacement rocker pillars in solid steel are also an acceptable modification but make sure that a true clamping action takes place on the rocker shaft to be fully effective.

O.H.C. Engines

Check cam bearings and see that caps are on original matched seatings. Light annular scoring is O.K. providing there is no evidence of hammering or lack of lubrication. Check fit of followers in head. If cam has been reground to smaller base circle, make sure that followers are not impinging on adjacent protruding bearing surfaces or other obstacles. Check clearance of cam lobe rotation in rocker box.

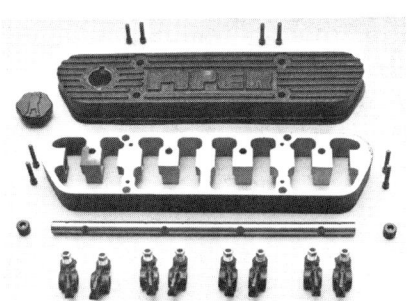
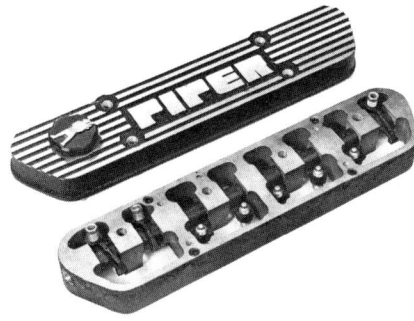

83. Integral rocker gear (in assembled and component form). Uses standard rockers and shaft.

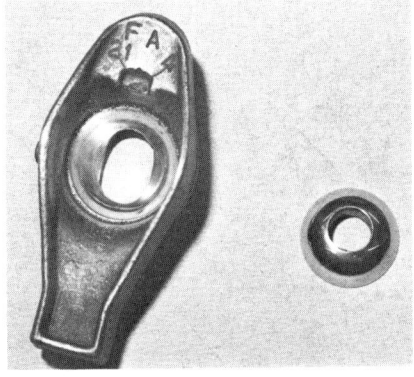

84. Ball and socket mounting for rocker arm (Ford V6).

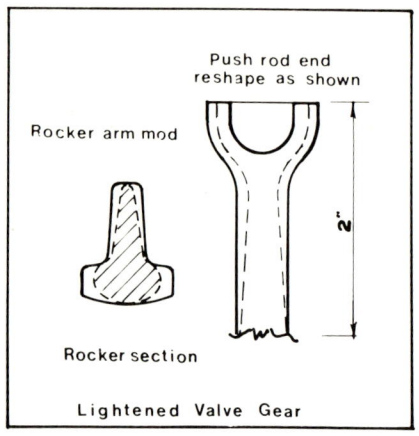

D31. *Lightened rocker arm and pushrod.*

Valve to valve and valve to piston clearance, hemispherical combustion chambers

Minimum valve to valve clearance at overlap T.D.C. should be 0.060 in. Remember, the inlet valve will be opening across the face of the exhaust, so the safe way to ensure clearance is to recess the exhaust and get it safely out of the path of the inlet.

Closest proximity of valve to piston will occur at approximately 10° B.T.D.C. for the exhaust and 10° A.T.D.C. for the inlet. Minimum clearance, valve to piston, should be 0.100 in., to allow for rod and piston stretch and also momentary variations in timing caused by over-revving. If pistons have to be pocketed, remember to check side clearance as well as face clearance.

Combustion chamber

Ensure that all sharp edges are broken and burrs removed. Check plug nose position when fully screwed home. There should be no spare threads in sight, either on the plug or the head. 'Run-out' threads, left by the tapping operation in the head, should be smoothed away. Any of these small protruberances can cause detonation.

Detonation

Detonation is secondary ignition, a result of inefficient combustion control, often started by superheated, glowing prominences in the combustion chamber. The pressure wave, generated by the detonating flame-spread, meets the flame-front of the normal ignition process somewhere in the centre of the chamber, and the resultant shock can cause severe damage, often witnessed as a hole in the piston crown. Detonation is audible at low speed as a dull crackle (not to be confused with the 'ping' of pinking, which is the harmless noise of over advance), but is often inaudible at high speed, at which point it can cause the most alarming damage.

Head and block faces and gasket should be treated as described in the turbocharging and supercharging section.

Deck height

The closest point that the piston crown comes to the head controls squish efficiency. Allow around 0.030 in. including allowance for head gasket etc. Any less than this may mean that the piston will touch the head as the rod stretches with inertia at high rpm.

Pistons and rings

It is essential to keep the piston as light as possible for reasons described later. With engines revving consistently over 8000rpm, the top ring should not be more than 0.040 in. wide, in order to keep its weight down. This is necessary

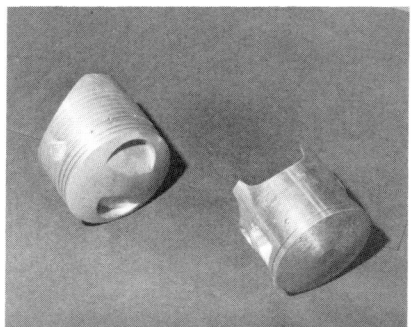

85. 4-stroke and 2-stroke pistons, showing single ring and lighter construction of 2-stroke piston.

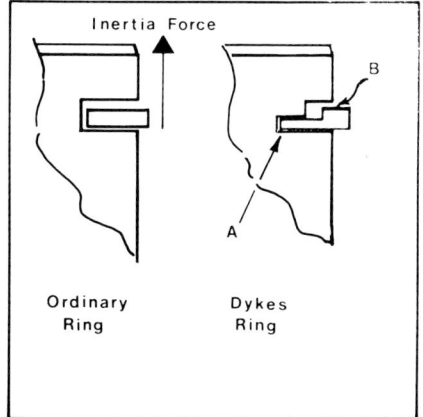

D32. Comparison of standard and 'Dykes' piston rings.

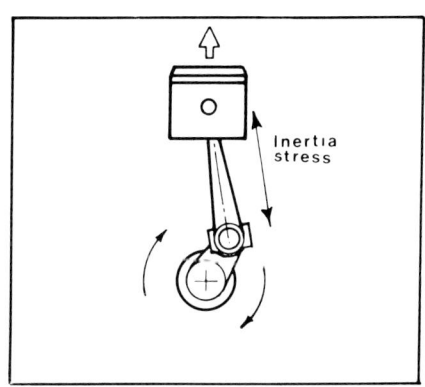

D33. Inertia stress in con-rod.

to prevent inertia sticking the ring to the top of the groove and preventing combustion pressure from getting down behind it to create the sealing pressure. This is also the reason for using a 'Dykes' ring (see D.32), which uses the horizontal section 'A' to hold to ring down, thus keeping the door open at 'B' to allow entry of gas pressure for sealing.

Unlike compression rings, the oil control ring should be a snug fit in the groove, ideally of simple two-piece bridge construction (Hepolite code MSO), but if not available, then three-piece (two slim rings with an expander between), but not pressure backed. Oil clearance should take place through drilled holes at the back of the groove and below the ring, at the top of the skirt.

Pistons with slotted grooves are not advisable for high speed use, due to potential failure at this point.

If forged pistons are available then these should be used, but only if the design is suitable. The old fashioned 'slipper' design, with two straight walls at right angles to the gudgeon pin and joining the thrust faces, is not desirable and does not make sufficient allowance for the expansion limits created by the wide operating temperature range of the modern engine.

The ideal piston is of 'jampot' or near circular design, with a generous skirt correctly ovalled and barrelled and, if forged, fully machined inside and out in order to reduce the excessive weight introduced by the necessary forging process that leaves solid metal above the gudgeon pin bosses internally. Cast piston designs avoid this problem and thus do not require internal machining.

Well designed and produced cast pistons are adequate for stages of tune up to Stage 3 as listed in the cam selection table on page 23.

Turbocharged engines

Generally the operating rpm range of these engines will be lower than that of naturally aspirated units. It is therefore not necessary to use ultra-light top compression rings: in fact a wider ring is desirable to lower the specific loading created by the excessive combustion pressures. For the same reasons it is not necessary for the piston to be of such lightweight construction.

These rules do not apply, however, for highly specialised engine designs conceived specifically as turbo full race power plants.

Connecting rods

Often the big villain of horrendous engine blow-ups, the con-rod can be a perfectly reliable component if its function is understood and the correct treatment given accordingly. Those who have dismantled both two-stroke and four-stroke engines will probably have noticed that the two-stroke rod is always of lighter construction.

The reason for this is the con-rod and piston, like all other bodies, exist in a state of inertia. Inertia is a resistance to any form of motion (often also found in many human beings!); that is, if they are moving, then they don't want to be speeded up or stopped, and if they are stationary, then they don't want to be moved. So, as the rod and piston reach the top of the exhaust stroke in a four-stroke engine, they want to carry on upwards but the crankshaft starts to pull them down. The two opposing forces try to stretch the rod and piston and create inertia stresses (See D.33).

Not generally realised is the fact that loads due to inertia in the four-stroke are considerably greater than loads due to combustion. For example, a

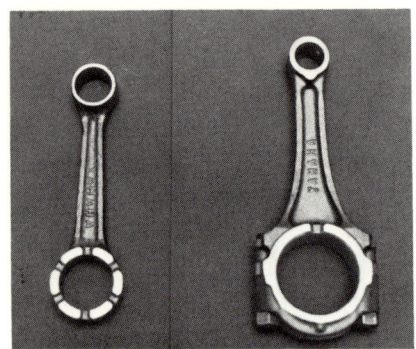

86. *2-stroke and 4-stroke con-rods. Showing greater size and strength of 4-stroke rod.*

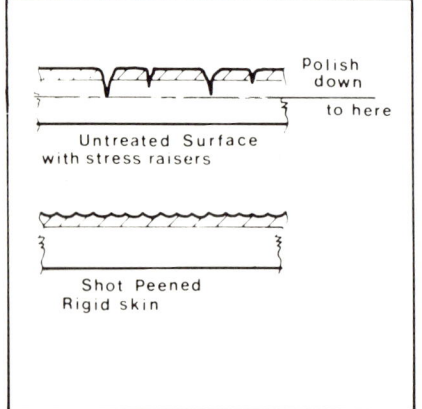

D34. *The effect of surface treatment.*

87. *Balancing 4-cylinder crankshaft.*

rod and piston that weigh a few pounds normally, will effectively weigh several thousand pounds at 10,000rpm. However, this weight is considerably offset at the top of the power stroke, by the cushioning effect of combustion pressure.

Now it becomes easier to understand why so many engine blow-ups take place on the overrun. With the throttle closed, the combustion cushion is lost and the components are being subjected to twice the number of inertia loads.

Of course, the same thing happens again at the bottom of the stroke, but this time the rod is in compression by the effective weight of the piston and the load is much easier to resist.

To sum up then, this is the usual sequence of con-rod failure. Inertia loads of rod and piston work on the big-end bolts, the bolts stretch or loosen, oil is lost from the big-end bearing, the bearing seizes and tears the rod apart somewhere between big and small end. On the next rotation, the broken rod end usually ventilates the block sideways. This is the usual failure, but if the big-end bearing is still intact and not blued, but the top of the rod is off, then that is due to inertia weight of the piston being too much for the rod design. *Moral:* If you're going to increase rpm, then keep piston weight to a minimum. Also, renew big-end bolts at regular intervals, torque them up carefully and don't use lockwashers of any kind. Use Loctite. Con-rods can also be further protected by having the flanks polished and shot-peened. This has the effect of removing stress raisers or potential breakage points and then adding a compressed, tough skin to improve its rigidity (see D.34).

The two-stroke con-rod is never subjected to this kind of treatment because, at the top of each stroke, it has the compression or combustion cushion, and, at the bottom of each stroke, it has the pumping cushion of the transfer process. Hence the lighter construction.

Crankshafts

Modern crankshafts are generally designed and constructed to withstand far heavier loads than the standard engine can impose. Consequently the level of tune can be lifted quite high, certainly to Stage 3, before a special purpose crank need even be considered.

A popular modern construction material is graphitic nodular iron, an alloy cast-iron of such high specification that it could be justifiably classified as a cast steel. This material has graphite inclusions that protrude at the machined surfaces to create an oil retaining finish of ideal characteristics. As produced, however, the graphite pockets can be left with sharp edges which can be removed by 'reverse lapping' the crank.

'Tuftriding', a high temperature surface treatment that introduces nitrogen to the surface layer, will also result in extending the high performance life of a standard crank.

Crank failures almost always occur at the fillet radii between journals and webs, so careful attention to these areas is critical when preparing the crank for assembly. The radii should be absolutely smooth and of generous size and can be improved by 'roll peening', a rather difficult but worthwhile process of work hardening and smoothing the standard finish.

However, the main cause of crank failure, apart from lubrication breakdown, is due to torsional vibration loads imposed by the transmission of uneven power pulses through an irregular shaped component. Production engine crankshafts are not as fully counterbalanced as they might be, due to cost and weight penalties and consequently they can never truly qualify as racing cranks. The latter are designed with full counterweighting for each cylinder assembly and are fully machined all over from high grade alloy steel forgings, thus reducing torsional vibrations to an acceptable minimum.

Crankshaft supports or main bearing caps in current engines are adequate for all requirements to Stage 5 in most cases, but support straps should be fitted to those older units that are still popular for tuning. The re-emerged but still competitive BL A-series in the Metro is an example.

Flywheel lightening

Often considered vital to good engine tuning and much misunderstood, the process of flywheel lightening is often quite unnecessary. Flywheel lightening cannot measurably improve power or acceleration. What it can do is to improve speed and smoothness of gearchanging for rally and circuit race cars so that is *appears* to enhance power output.

The engineering explanation of this is quite simple ... As the weight of individual components is reduced so the power needed to accelerate them is reduced or, for any given power, the rate of acceleration is higher. But compared to the total weight of a complete vehicle, even a lightweight single seater racing car, the reduction in flywheel weight is insignificant, so the improvement in vehicle performance is immeasurably small, and gets even smaller as the vehicle weight increases to that of a road car.

So it is unlikely that the cost of flywheel lightening will produce any worthwhile return other than the pleasure of a lumpy and unreliable tickover created by the reduction in 'flywheel effect'.

In the event that the decision is taken to lighten the flywheel, the job should be taken to an expert in order to get optimum weight removed, *ie* as close to the periphery as possible, for maximum effect, but leaving sufficient material to support the ring-gear and avoid distortion due to clutch load and heat dissipation. Alternatively the production cast-iron flywheel can be replaced by a lightweight steel component.

WARNING! Indiscriminate lightening of a flywheel can be damaging to your health.

88. Balancing a connecting rod.

Balancing

All modern production engines are balanced to a degree, but fine balancing should be carried out as well. Balance pistons weight for weight including rings and pin. Balance rods so that all big-ends weigh the same and correct small ends as near as sensibly possible. Dynamically balance crank, including flywheel and clutch, but *not* including the centre-plate. Don't forget to mark flywheel to clutch positions for re-assembly.

Double check crank alignment on two-strokes together with crankcase seals and gaskets, to ensure high crankcase efficiency.

89. Easy rotation by hand of assembled engine.

Assembly hints

Double check all oilways for cleanliness, even the difficult ones. They had to be drilled somehow, so there must be an access plug.

During assembly, make sure all parts move freely. Even a four-cylinder bottom end with pistons in should be rotatable by hand effort alone, without the use of a bar.

Make sure oil-pump, relief system and filtration are in perfect condition. The engine relies on an oil cushion between all running surfaces, particularly bearing shells and pins. Any metal to metal contact will cause instant failure.